About This Book

Why is this book important?

A competent job analysis is the foundation of all other human resource functions. If we do not understand the nature of the job to be done, we cannot select appropriate candidates for that job, assess their worth in the job market, develop appropriate training and development programs, mentor them, or adequately carry out any of the multitudinous HR functions. It all must begin with a proper job analysis, a task for which this book provides a comprehensive guide.

What can you expect from this book?

This book provides the reader with a context for understanding the importance of doing a proper job analysis together with a step-by-step guide to conducting such an analysis. One unique element of this guide is a series of eight templates that provide the basis for conducting job analyses for eight different levels of job families, from the entry-level to the senior manager/executive. HR professionals or line managers can readily use these templates with confidence that they have the necessary tools as well as the understanding of the context of this process.

How is this book organized?

Beginning with two chapters on the context and importance of doing a competent job analysis, the book provides guides to specifying the work activities of tasks that make up the job, identifying the competencies necessary to successfully perform that job, spelling out the unique characteristics of the workplace in which the job will be performed, and finally, specifying the performance level at which this job needs to be executed. The templates or instruments necessary to complete each of the elements of a thorough job analysis are provided in an appendix and on a website (*www.pfeiffer.com/go/LeonardGoodstein*). This provides a convenient way that they easily can be customized for use in doing a job analysis.

About Pfeiffer

Pfeiffer serves the professional development and hands-on resource needs of training and human resource practitioners and gives them products to do their jobs better. We deliver proven ideas and solutions from experts in HR development and HR management, and we offer effective and customizable tools to improve workplace performance. From novice to seasoned professional, Pfeiffer is the source you can trust to make yourself and your organization more successful.

Essential Knowledge Pfeiffer produces insightful, practical, and comprehensive materials on topics that matter the most to training and HR professionals. Our Essential Knowledge resources translate the expertise of seasoned professionals into practical, how-to guidance on critical workplace issues and problems. These resources are supported by case studies, worksheets, and job aids and are frequently supplemented with CD-ROMs, websites, and other means of making the content easier to read, understand, and use.

Essential Tools Pfeiffer's Essential Tools resources save time and expense by offering proven, ready-to-use materials—including exercises, activities, games, instruments, and assessments—for use during a training or team-learning event. These resources are frequently offered in looseleaf or CD-ROM format to facilitate copying and customization of the material.

Pfeiffer also recognizes the remarkable power of new technologies in expanding the reach and effectiveness of training. While e-hype has often created whizbang solutions in search of a problem, we are dedicated to bringing convenience and enhancements to proven training solutions. All our e-tools comply with rigorous functionality standards. The most appropriate technology wrapped around essential content yields the perfect solution for today's on-the-go trainers and human resource professionals.

Pfeiffer
www.pfeiffer.com

Essential resources for training and HR professionals

Our readers are invited to view and download the templates and instruments from the appendices of this book. The materials can be customized for use in doing a job analysis. The materials are available FREE with the purchase of this book at www.pfeiffer.com/go/LeonardGoodstein.

A Practical Guide to Job Analysis

Erich P. Prien,
Leonard D. Goodstein,
Jeanette Goodstein,
and Louis G. Gamble, Jr.

Pfeiffer
A Wiley Imprint
www.pfeiffer.com

Published by Pfeiffer
An Imprint of Wiley
989 Market Street, San Francisco, CA 94103-1741   www.pfeiffer.com

For additional copies/bulk purchases of this book in the U.S. please contact 800-274-4434.

Pfeiffer books and products are available through most bookstores. To contact Pfeiffer directly call our Customer Care Department within the U.S. at 800-274-4434, outside the U.S. at 317-572-3985, fax 317-572-4002, or visit www.pfeiffer.com.

Pfeiffer also publishes its books in a variety of electronic formats. Some content that appears in print may not be available in electronic books.

Library of Congress Cataloging-in-Publication Data

A practical guide to job analysis / Erich P. Prien ... [et al.].
    p. cm.
  Includes bibliographical references and index.
  ISBN 978-0-470-43444-4 (cloth)
  1. Job analysis. I. Prien, Erich P.,
  HF5549.5.J6P73 2009
  658.3'06 -dc22

                                          2008051523

Acquiring Editor: Matthew Davis   Editorial Assistant: Lindsay Morton
Director of Development: Kathleen Dolan Davies   Manufacturing Supervisor: Becky Morgan
Production Editor: Dawn Kilgore
Editor: Rebecca Taff

Printed in the United States of America

Printing   10 9 8 7 6 5 4 3 2 1

Contents

*All Appendices are available for free download at
www.pfeiffer.com/go/LeonardGoodstein

Preface

This workbook was written with three audiences in mind. The first audience is the relatively new human resource (HR) professional who needs to develop an understanding of the procedures and methodology of job analysis in order to conduct such analyses and then use the data from such analyses in their daily work. The second audience is the experienced HR professional who is trained and experienced in job analysis but who can use specialized information about specific methods and approaches for conducting job analyses, applying the results of such analyses, and training and supervising more junior members of the HR staff. A third audience is line managers who are interested in understanding how competent job analyses can improve the quality of the workforce and positively impact the bottom line.

The organization of this workbook follows the sequence in which job analyses are conducted. The introductory chapter places job analyses in the context of the process of the management of the organization's most important asset—its human capital. In the second chapter we discuss in some depth what is involved in job analyses, including some caveats and cautions to observe. Chapter Three provides a detailed description of how to perform a job analysis. The next chapter provides information on how to use the eight generic job analyses that are, to our knowledge, unique contributions to the field. Each of these eight generic job analyses then follows in a separate section, arranged in order of increasing complexity of the job from entry-level jobs to managerial positions. But work is always done in an organization, and the nature of that organization—its unique culture, strategy, and structure—provides a context within which work is performed. No job analysis is complete without understanding the characteristics of that workplace. The next chapter provides an overview for understanding those characteristics and introduced our Workplace Characteristics Profile (WCP), a newly revised instrument for identifying the specific characteristics of a workplace that directly impact job performance. Our final chapter deals with how the various levels of job performance can and should be established. Thus we provide a comprehensive manual for performing a job analysis.

Our focus is always on identifying and specifying the particular tasks involved in effectively performing an identified job and the necessary competencies required to do that job. Such a focus is required to produce narrative job descriptions that can be used successfully in recruiting, screening, selecting, and integrating new employees into the workforce.

Although job analyses have been conducted on a systematic basis in business and industry for many decades, for the most part they have not led to producing job descriptions that effectively communicate to others the competencies required to fill those jobs successfully. It seems to us that many of these earlier job descriptions were not written with sufficient attention to how the information included was to be used. All too often, the focus was on describing the tasks involved in the job, rather than on the competencies necessary to carry out the tasks. This focus left the end-user of the job description having to interpret the competencies required for success from the narrative description. The approach of this workbook is to obviate the need for such interpretation. The model of job analysis presented here produces both a clear statement of the work activities involved in the job *and* the knowledge, skills, and abilities required for successful performance of that job.

In conventional job analyses the individual(s) responsible for performing the analysis must begin with an examination of the tasks involved, and then determine the knowledge, skills, and abilities necessary to perform those tasks; this analysis leads to a job description that typically will combine similar tasks and then separately identify the necessary competencies to perform each set of tasks. This resultant job description serves as a template for this specific job and others in that job family.

In order to circumvent this time- and labor-intensive process, we have developed eight standardized questionnaires that ask respondents first to rate the relative importance of each of a series of work activities involved in a particular job family provided in a list and, second, to rate the importance of a separate set of competencies known to be involved in the successful completion of those work activities. Compiling both these ratings of the importance of various work activities and of the associated competencies produces a job description based on quantitative ratings that identify the required competencies.

Considerable prior work in developing standardized job analysis questionnaires does exist, but all of these efforts have focused on producing a single set of work activities and competencies (e.g., Fleishman, 1992). While there is merit in having a single instrument that covers the entire range of jobs, we firmly believe that such a single-minded approach cannot do justice to the enormous range of jobs and competencies necessary in today's increasingly complex workplace. Chapter Four addresses these issues in greater depth.

Any work of this scope involves the efforts of several others besides the authors. We extend our sincere appreciation to Dr. Kristin Prien for her technical assistance and, even more importantly, her support and affection. Rebecca Taff provided her usual editorial expertise to producing a final product, for which we are exceedingly grateful.

1

AN INTRODUCTION TO JOB ANALYSIS

Identifying the right person to fill a job vacancy has always been difficult. Our aging, culturally diverse, and heterogeneous workforce has increased that difficulty, and our globally competitive economy makes searching for competent workers an even more formidable task. The rise of the Internet and the virtual avalanche of resumes employers receive in response to each job posting make the task of finding suitable candidates yet more laborious.

Still, hiring the wrong people poses serious risks to all businesses—from the smallest to the large, multinational corporation. Indeed, the costs of a hiring mistake are estimated to be from one-half to ten times an individual's yearly salary. The expense of hiring mistakes must be controlled by using a systematic and consistent approach to identifying and hiring competent and suitable people.

Hiring a competent and suitable individual to fill a position is a true win-win proposition—a win for both the new employee and the employer. Recruiting competent people for positions in which they can succeed, feel good about what they are doing, and experience the positive regard of their co-workers is highly reinforcing to everybody. New employees should experience a boost in their sense of self-worth and self-esteem. They should begin to feel secure and bring greater focus and energy to their work, as job satisfaction increases. This growing sense of achievement and capability, in turn, leads to greater increases in motivation, to further achievement, and to a greater sense of competence.

Why Do We Analyze Jobs?

Completing a competent job analysis is ordinarily necessary in order to write the job description, the formal statement of the responsibilities involved, and the qualities necessary for success on this specific job. Without such a job analysis, it is difficult, if not impossible, to prepare a useful job description—and without a job description it would be impossible to fill any job vacancy successfully. A sample job description is included as Appendix A.

But job descriptions have a bad reputation in most organizations. Both employees and managers regard writing job descriptions as a waste of time—until they need to use the information from that job description. Many feel that job descriptions are too confining, that they limit people to a specific set of tasks, and that they limit the behavior of job incumbents. Consequently, writing job analyses is one part of human capital management that everyone loves to hate, arguably even more than performance reviews. People give various reasons for not wanting to do (or even be involved in preparing) job descriptions:

- "It's too much work, and I have more important things to do."
- "It's a waste of time; my people know what their jobs are."
- "Our jobs change too fast to write descriptions."
- "A job description is too confining. I want my people to be flexible."

However, the information obtained from job analyses and which leads to the job description is essential for virtually all of the other human resources (HR) functions. The manager who does not have time to work on job descriptions today certainly doesn't have time to defend against an EEO suit later. Perhaps the current employees really do know what their jobs are, but what happens when a key employee suddenly leaves, and the information necessary for recruiting a replacement is not there? And if jobs are changing rapidly, knowing what skills are needed to perform these jobs is even more essential, since training people in the newly necessary skills will be a constant requirement. Finally, while flexibility is good in the abstract, organizations require a functional level of responsibility and accountability, which requires job descriptions, which in turn require competent job analyses. Thus, the job description should include information about the duties the employee performs, the knowledge, skills, and abilities, that is, the competencies, necessary to perform those tasks, and any other job-related information. Nowhere is this more important than in the hiring process.

The Hiring Process

For the employer, hiring such people is equally important. First, it saves money by raising productivity, lowering personnel turnover, and reducing supervisory problems. Further, personnel conflicts and problems decline sharply, as does the turnover of new hires, all of which result in considerable savings in additional hiring costs and downtime. Proper selection processes significantly reduce the risk of litigation for negligent or discriminatory hiring practices. An organization succeeds when its hiring process places people in jobs that allow them to utilize their abilities, capabilities, and skills. Finally, from a societal point of view, good selection also provides genuine equal opportunity to all people and helps our economy grow by increasing productivity and reducing job dissatisfaction.

Despite the many benefits of hiring the right candidate to fill a job vacancy, doing so is rarely easy for most organizations. In our experience, one of the most important reasons for this difficulty is that all too many supervisors and managers do not have a clear understanding of the competencies necessary for success in that job and how to assess those competencies. If you do not know what you are looking for, it is difficult to find it!

Prior to an in-depth analysis of job analysis, it is important to place job analysis in a proper context, one that illuminates its importance in the management of an organization's most important asset, its human capital.

The Human Capital Life Cycle

We believe that the ideal human capital life cycle is best understood as involving six more or less discrete steps. All too often employers do not differentiate these steps clearly and thus do not follow them, leading to poor-quality outcomes. The six steps approach employee recruitment, selection, and hiring as the initial aspects of an employee life cycle, one that is concerned with employees throughout their employment careers. The six steps are

- Job analysis
- Recruitment
- Screening
- Final selection
- Job orientation
- Training and development

Additional phases of human capital management appear later in work life as employees move through a career and into retirement, but we will concern ourselves only with these initial six steps, ones that build on the job analysis and universally affect virtually all employees and most jobs. Beginning with job analysis, we will review each of these steps briefly.

Job Analysis

It is not possible to overestimate the importance of a competent job analysis in the human capital process. It is the step on which the entire employee life cycle hinges and thus should be regarded as one of the most important professional responsibilities of both the human resource staff who must conduct thorough job analyses and of their managers who must initiate and oversee the process.

Simply stated, the purpose of a job analysis is to provide an in-depth understanding of the competencies required for success in order to select appropriate candidates. A job competency is a behavior, or set of behaviors, necessary to accomplish a specific work task or achieve a specific goal. These competencies can range from the most simple, such as filing, operating a punch press, or answering callers politely and warmly, to the most complex, such as neurosurgery or getting along with a difficult supervisor.

The importance of using comprehensive job analyses in selecting among candidates is strongly supported by empirical research. This research (e.g., Campion, Palmer, & Campion, 1997; Campion, Pursell, & Brown, 1988;) clearly shows that, when the hiring process was based on a careful job analysis, the prediction of job success is greatly increased, and that it is possible to identify correctly those candidates most likely to succeed. This line of research also supports the conclusion that much of the early research on the problems in predicting job success was seriously flawed by one critical omission—the lack of job analyses that identified the characteristics necessary for success on that job. While the following chapters of this book are concerned with the nuts and bolts of conducting a competent job analysis, the remainder of this chapter will continue with the importance of using job analyses throughout the employee life cycle.

Recruitment

In job postings for recruiting candidates, the job analysis should be used to clearly specify clearly the knowledge, skills, and abilities (competencies) of successful candidates. Although this will probably not reduce the flood of resumes that recruiters currently experience with every job posting, it does serve two important purposes: First, it provides a template for screening the mass of resumes. Which of these resumes clearly indicates that the sender possesses the requirements necessary for success? For example, to what extent has the applicant tailored the resume to fit the articulated set of requirements in the job posting? How carefully has the resume been prepared? How often have there been job changes? What is the nature of the self-described accomplishments?

Second, an accurate and sufficiently detailed posting will serve as a template that gives a measure of protection against charges of discriminatory hiring. The degree to which the applicant does not meet the specific requirements set forth in the job posting is critical in any defense against discriminatory hiring practices, providing that it can be shown that these requirements are actually related to on-the-job success, a topic to which we return later.

If the initial recruitment process includes some interviewing, the recruiter needs to remember that this interview has two purposes. One is to sell the job to attractive candidates, those who appear to have the necessary set of requirements. The other is to verify that the applicant does have the requirements. This means that the recruiter must understand both the job and the candidate well enough to probe for the validity of the information contained in the resume. Deciding whether or not the recruiter knows enough about the job to test the requirements should be an important factor in selecting recruiters for specific jobs.

One of the dangers of conducting initial interviews of this type is that the recruiter may view the purpose solely as selling the candidate on the job. Organizations should be careful not to reward recruiters for the number of candidates they promote to the screening process. Rewarding recruiters for the number of candidates who make it through the screening process to the final selection stage is far wiser.

Screening

Most hiring organizations do not make a clear distinction between screening and selection, which means that the organization is putting too much time, effort, and energy into examining too many inappropriate candidates. By screening we mean the identification of those few applicants who appear most likely to possess the requirements for advancement to the selection process. We would argue that the optimal number of such candidates who should be advanced to the final selection process is between three and five.

Final Selection

This final selection among the best three to five candidates will ordinarily involve a series of interviews with different key supervisors and managers in the organization. All too often the final selection process tends to be unplanned, which leads to non-functional redundancy in the topics addressed. We strongly recommend that the persons who will be conducting the interviews meet prior to the first interview and develop an interview plan based on the job analysis; for example, decide who will ask what questions, decide which issues need to be covered by more than one interviewer, and so forth. Such planning greatly increases the database developed by the interview process, and also makes the candidate feel that, if this is a sample of management behavior, the organization is well managed.

In addition, an in-depth follow-up and verification of each candidate's education, work history, and background should occur in order to determine if the candidate possesses the essential requirements. Our experience revealed that there are too many cases of falsified educational records, non-existent jobs, bankruptcies, convictions for a variety of offenses, and other misdeeds, none of which were included in the resume, of course. Research has shown that in most resumes as many as one-third of all the so-called "facts" are simply not true. Each of these issues needs to be carefully checked.

This final step of the selection process that we are advocating requires time and effort, but it has the capacity to pay rich dividends in the kind of employee that it yields. Indeed, the same can be said of the entire hiring process that we have described thus far. There is a clear rule at work here: "Hire hard, and manage easy!" The reverse, however, seems to be more often the rule.

Job Orientation

Most descriptions of the initial human capital management process do not include job orientation as part of this process, but we insist that they should do so. Most frequently, orientation involves simply turning the new hire over to the human resources staff, who spend their time explaining the various company benefit programs and having the new hire fill out the necessary forms. While these are important ingredients of any orientation program, they are not the issues that are paramount to most new employees.

What new employees really want to know and should be told is how to succeed on the job and how to avoid getting in difficulties early on. Two questions we often suggest the supervisor should answer as if the new employee were asking them are: "If your best friend were to come to work here, what bit of advice would you offer about how to succeed?" and "What could I do in the short run that would cause me to fail?" This is clearly the advice that one would give to a close friend or relative, but is often very difficult for a new employee to obtain. And this advice should be based on the data developed through the job analysis.

In our judgment, the hiring process does not end with the final selection decision. After that decision is made, every organization should want the successful candidate to succeed. A job orientation that provides psychological support as well as administrative support enhances the likelihood of that success, as does having a training and development plan in place for the new employee, one based on the job analysis.

Training and Development

Once the new employee is oriented and working toward becoming successful, the issue of the employee's needs for further training and development become important. When a new employee is hired as a trainee, the importance of a training and development plan should be obvious—a plan ready to be implemented should be available. Indeed, virtually all new employees will have training and development needs—needs that the job analysis and the selection process should have highlighted.

Because there are no perfect new hires, each will pose some kind of unique needs for further training and development, and it is at this early stage that these needs should be addressed. While obviously other training and development needs will surface over time, the new hire offers a unique opportunity for training and development. What are this new hire's specific training needs? Where could a training program, a course, some coaching, or mentoring early on make a real difference in performance and enhance the possibilities for long-term success? Further, this kind of effort on the part of organization is likely to make a real difference in the attitude of the new employee. "Someone up there really wants me to succeed!"

That the job analysis is the cornerstone of every employee life cycle process should be obvious, as should the fact that it affects applicants, new hires, employees, and employers. In every instance, the job analysis is the core of the process, from identifying what requirements are necessary to developing training and development plans for individual employees as well as in supporting and mentoring them to become successful parts of a well-functioning organization Ployhart, Schneider, & Schmitt, 2006).

In summary, we have sketched out a human capital management process that provides a context for understanding the important role competent job analyses play in that process, and we now turn to an in-depth look at what is involved in job analyses.

2

WHAT IS A JOB ANALYSIS?

Defining Job Analysis

Human capital management in organizations virtually always requires an in-depth understanding of the work that people do in that organization. The process by which this understanding is developed is a *job analysis*; a *job description* is the documentation of the results of that analysis. While these two terms are often used interchangeably, we strongly recommend against such usage, as job analysis is a process and a job description is a product of that process. Simply put, a job analysis is a *systematic process* for collecting and analyzing information about a job.

In a more comprehensive and detailed definition, Harvey (1991) defined job analysis as "the collection of data on (a) 'job-oriented' behavior, such as job tasks and work procedures; (b) more abstract 'worker-oriented' behavior, such as decision making, supervision, and information processing; (c) behaviors involved in interactions with machines, materials, and tools; (d) methods of evaluating performance, such as productivity and error rates; (e) job context, such as working conditions and type of compensation systems; and (f) personnel requirements, such as skills, physical ability, and personality traits" (p. 74.) This definition of job analysis focuses on the systematic collection of data on the observable job behaviors of employees and what is accomplished by these behaviors and what technologies are required to do so. A second aspect focuses on the work environment in which the employees function. While not every job analysis involves all of these components, Harvey's definition does articulate the parameters of job analysis. Those interested will find that Wilson's (2007) comprehensive history of the development of job analysis provides a context for better understanding these definitional issues.

Job analysis has further been codified by the *Uniform Guidelines on Employee Selection Procedures* (1978), designed by the U.S. Government to assist employers and others to comply with Federal law prohibiting discriminatory employment practices on the grounds of race, color, religion, sex, or national origin. The *Guidelines* specify, "Job analysis ... includes an analysis of the important work behavior(s) required for successful performance and their relative importance and, if the behavior results in work product(s), an analysis of the work product(s). Any job analysis should focus on the work behavior(s) and the tasks associated with them. If work behavior(s) are not observable, the job analysis should identify and analyze those aspects of the behavior(s) that can be observed and the work products" (section 1607, 14.C.2.) The purpose of these *Guidelines* is to provide a framework for determining the proper use of tests and other selection procedures. The many cases that have been based on allegations of violations of these *Guidelines* provide ample evidence that employers who fail to conform to them do so at their own peril.

Given the importance that job analyses play in the management of human capital, it is surprising that job analyses are not regarded as a more critical tool in the field of human resources. Over three decades ago, Prien (1977) observed, "Although job analysis is an essential feature of every activity engaged in by industrial-organizational psychologists, the subject is treated in most textbooks in a manner which suggests that any fool can do it and thus is a task which can be delegated to the lowest level technician" (p. 167). Unfortunately, the situation has not much changed, and this important function is not given the proper degree of attention and respect either by psychologists or HR professionals.

Applications of Job Analyses

A variety of important reasons support conducting job analyses in the workplace. These include recruitment, candidate selection, employee training and development, performance management, organizational management and planning, and litigation protection. Each of these will be briefly reviewed.

Recruitment

The first external application of job analysis is in recruitment, when the job description becomes the basis for recruiting applicants. In beginning to fill a vacant job, the recruiter needs to know the job responsibilities as well as the skills and other characteristics required of candidates. Not only is it necessary for the recruiter to know these things, but candidates need to know the kind of job for which they are applying. The need for a job description should be obvious to all.

Candidate Selection

In our experience, candidate selection accounts for most job analyses. Employers need to know in some detail the work activities involved in each job vacancy and, most importantly, the knowledge, skills, and abilities—the competencies—required to fill that job successfully. While most employers maintain files of job descriptions, there is widespread understanding that many, if not most, of these job descriptions are dated and need to be redone, especially for jobs deemed to be critically important.

The work activities of a job change over time, as do the requirements for successfully carrying out those activities. As an example, consider the impact that the computer has had on the work activities both in the office and on the shop floor. Administrative positions that once had a heavy dose of taking shorthand and transcription are now given over to a very different set of activities, ones that require a rather different set of requirements. Similarly, the introduction of the computer onto the shop floor and into the warehouse has produced an equally large impact on the work activities. The tightening of bolts on the assembly line is now done by a computer-driven robot, the contents of the warehouse are all bar coded, and most jobs require computer skills for success. Such changes are ongoing and have enormous impact on the competency requirements for hiring. And these changes can be specified only by a careful job analysis.

Further, it is important to recognize that many skills are specific to a given occupation (Reiter-Palmer, Young, Strange, Manning, & James, 2006) and that these occupationally specific skills are only be identified by a job analysis.

One use of job analyses is in developing behavioral interviewing protocols for candidate screening. The job description that is the end-product of the job analysis should provide a clear picture of the work and activities and the requirements. These then should provide the basis on which to develop a behavioral interviewing protocol—questions inquiring into a candidate's experience in such work activities and seeking to establish the degree to which the candidate has the necessary requirements to perform the important work activities. This is a method for developing a behavioral interview much preferred to the more generic approach that lacks a specific job-relevant focus.

Another important use of job analyses is as the criteria for validity studies of any pre-employment selection procedure, especially psychological tests. The *Standards for Educational and Psychological Testing* (American Educational Research Association and others, 1999) specify that the job requirements involved in studies of predictor-criteria relationships should be "determined by a job analysis" (p. 160). In other words, the validity of a psychological test or any procedure for selecting job candidates must be determined by the correlation of that procedure with an important aspect of job performance as identified by a job analysis.

Employee Training and Development

Once a current job analysis becomes available, the competency of current employees in that job becomes apparent. Employees without a high level of the identified necessary competencies will be less productive than they otherwise should be. For example, if a new applicant tracking system is introduced in the HR function, someone has to be hired to manage that system. But, implicit in that decision, is the question of the competency of the existing HR staff to use that new system. Without knowing the answer to that question, the positive impact of the introduction of this new system will be less than intended. Thus, the job analysis used for the new hire should lead to an analysis of the competencies of the existing staff, and a training and development program should be instituted to produce the necessary competencies.

The job analysis can impact on the individual training and development level as well. It is rare that even those candidates who are the best fit developed through the job analysis are a *perfect fit*. The selection process should have identified both the candidate's strengths—those that led to the selection—and weaknesses—those that need to be addressed by some training and development process. This might be part of a supervisory or mentoring process or by some actual training, either on the job or somewhere else. In a somewhat dated example, a very experienced travel agent with an established clientele was hired by a large travel agency. The agent, despite her considerable experience, has little experience using Sabre Travel Network®, the computer booking system that had been identified as an important requirement in the job analysis. Her experience and list of clients were sufficient to outweigh her lack of skill with Sabre, a lack that could be remedied by taking a week-long training course, which was an acceptable solution to both parties. Clearly in this case, as in all training decisions, the job analysis is the starting point.

Performance Management

Another important use of job analysis is in performance management. Job analyses play an important role in developing or modifying compensation systems and in performance appraisal. Determining the various levels of performance on a given job is an essential aspect of every job analysis. The knowledge of what constitutes an outstanding level of performance, an average level, and a borderline level is a critical aspect of performance management and should be the basis for setting pay and bonuses, the need for training and development, and for virtually all other aspects of the HR function.

Job analyses have been used not only to set pay levels but also to help determine whether different jobs require different requirements or effort, or involve different working conditions. In either case, such differences merit different pay scales. Jobs that involve equivalent factors, however, should lead to equal pay.

The pay level a job warrants is also important, and the job characteristics as determined by the job analysis are frequently used to determine the level of pay. Among the factors included in such decisions are

- Level of education, training, or experience required
- Degree of creativity involved
- Strength or stamina necessary
- Amount of responsibility
- Degree of independence of action
- Scope of influence
- Intellectual demands, including problem solving
- Risk of death, injury, or sickness

Presumably the level of each of these factors can be identified by a job analysis and then combined in some meaningful way to determine the level of the job among the various jobs in that organization. The job description and the combined evaluation of these various factors provide the basis for establishing a compensation system that is then priced according to the data produced by a salary survey of similar jobs in the local job market.

Since such comparisons are fraught with uncertainties, they have become the basis of a considerable amount of litigation about the equality of pay for different jobs. As just one example of the ambiguities involved, consider the difficulties inherent in attempting to use job analysis to justify equal pay of elementary school teachers and truck drivers. While there is some evidence that sophisticated statistical analysis of the results of job analyses can be used successfully to predict market compensation rates (Harvey, 1991, pp. 144–146), this can be done only for blue-collar jobs. Further, it is often argued that such an approach captures only existing discriminatory pay polices and does little to advance the cause of equal pay for equal work. It is safe to conclude that setting compensation systems on the basis of job analysis is a complex and difficult process.

Job analyses are also used in the performance appraisal process. For this process, job analyses should highlight the various work activities involved in performing a job and the relative importance of each activity. A rational performance appraisal system would evaluate the quality of the work performed by the individual being appraised according to the various importance ratings. It should be far more critical for that employee being rated to perform the important tasks more competently than for him or her to perform those of lesser importance competently. Unfortunately, this does not always seem to be the case, and often employees feel that they are downgraded for not attending to rather trivial tasks, ones not critical to fulfilling the organization's mission. This leads to a feeling on the part of employees that the performance appraisal process is an unimportant managerial task, so they often discount the entire process.

Organizational Management and Planning

As we noted above, the appropriateness of job descriptions tends to decay over time. Changes in the marketplace require new behaviors, technology changes jobs with warp speed, and incumbents begin to do their jobs in idiosyncratic ways. As a result of these and other changes, job descriptions become obsolete. Further, mergers and acquisitions lead to a need to integrate different human resources management systems. And a new CEO comes in and decides to rationalize the HR function, to update the job descriptions, create a new compensation system, one based on equal pay for equal work, none of which can be accomplished without starting with a job analysis.

When one of us became the CEO of a large professional association, he quickly learned about employee discontent over what appeared to be favoritism in assigning job titles, compensation, and a variety of other benefits. It appeared that the only way to deal with this unrest was through an organization-wide review and rationalization, beginning with job analyses. To win employee acceptance of the process, the staff was promised that no one would suffer financially or in status.

The organization had almost five hundred employees, and the HR function was inadequate to perform the required work. A national HR consulting firm was engaged to create an organization-wide series of job analyses, draft current job descriptions based on these analyses, create a uniform set of job titles, and recommend a compensation system based on the job content involved and a regional salary survey. This was done over a period of several months and was widely accepted by both rank-and-file employees and the organization's board of directors. Moreover, this work enabled the organization to identify where additional resources were needed and where redundancy would provide some resources to fill those gaps. But all of this depended on the first step—the job analyses.

Litigation Protection

Still another use of job analyses is to reduce an organization's exposure to litigation based on allegations of discriminatory hiring practices. In order to ensure that all individuals are treated fairly in the workplace, including in hiring, pay, training, and other conditions of employment, we need to base all of our decisions on job-related qualifications. The only way to be able to do this is through the use of job analyses. For example, if we wish to hire a plumber, we need to ascertain that applicants can run pipe and have a license to do so, requirements based on the job analysis. Simply stated, if we are to hire people based on the qualifications to perform a job, we first must determine what those requirements for doing that job are—and conducting a job analysis is the only legal way to do this.

As we noted above, the Uniform Guidelines are quite explicit in requiring "an analysis of important work behaviors required for successful performance" as the basis for any hiring action. Any selection process should begin with such a job analysis that establishes the criteria against which applicants should be compared. Further, the job analysis establishes the criteria for establishing the validity of any assessment measure to be used in the selection process. Goodstein and Prien (2006) provide a more detailed discussion of the use of criteria to establish the validity of psychological tests and a catalogue of commonly used tests.

While there is no absolute or certain shield against litigation, basing selection decisions on a careful, thorough, and current job analysis and using only well-validated selection procedures based on those job analyses will go a long way to deter frivolous filings. One additional point is the critical importance of a careful, contemporaneous record documenting what was done and why it was done. In our experience, one of the major problems that our clients experience in defending themselves in HR litigation is the failure to document properly what was done.

This catalogue of the uses of job analyses is far from complete, as we have not included the use of job analyses in research on the nature of work and how work is changing, studies of the structure of work, and so on. But the focus of this book is on providing useful tools for the practicing HR professional and such conceptually focused research is of little practical use to this audience.

Elements of a Job Analysis

Traditional job analysis has four typical components:

1. A description of the work activity (WA) or tasks involved in doing the job;
2. The knowledge, skills, and abilities (KSA) or competencies necessary to perform the job;
3. Data on the range of job performance; and
4. The characteristics of the workplace.

The data contained in these four components provide the basis for drafting the job description, which should provide an integrated narrative picture of the job and what is required to fill that job successfully.

Work Activity (WA)

The process of a job analysis typically begins with a description of the major job functions, the activities in which a job incumbent regularly engages—the reasons why the job exists. One inherent problem in describing work activities is the level at which the activity is described. At the most basic level are the job *elements*, "the smallest unit into which work can be divided without analyzing separate motions, movement, and mental processes" (Cascio, 1987, p. 185.)

A more useful approach is that of *Functional Job Analysis* (Fine, 1989, Fine & Cronshaw, 1999), which specifies (1) an action verb, which describes the action performed in observable terms; (2) the outcomes or results of that action; (3) the tools or other equipment used; and (4) the amount of discretion allowed the worker in that action. Two examples should serve to clarify some of the issues in this approach to WA. In the first, "The assembler takes one end of the red wire and one end of the green wire and joins them together with a screw nut." In the second, "The surgeon takes the scalpel and makes a long incision into the chest of the comatose patient." In both examples, the action is described clearly, the tools involved are specified, the outcomes are clear, and the level of discretion is implicit and very different. These examples represent both the approach and content of the approach, sometimes referred to as *major job requirements*, to describing the WA that we advocate.

There two aspects to the WA process: one is the importance of the action to the success of performing the job and the other is the frequency with which that action is performed. Obviously, important and frequent actions constitute the bulk of the WA. But important but infrequent actions often need to be included. For example, while most police officers never draw and fire their handguns in the course of their careers, when such action is required it is critical to the success of that job. Thus, descriptions of WA should identify both the importance and frequency of actions, especially when highly important WA occur infrequently.

Knowledge, Skills, and Ability (KSA)

The second question that every job analysis must address concerns the knowledge, skills, and abilities (KSA) or competencies necessary to perform these WA. *Knowledge* is defined as an organized body of information, usually of a factual or procedural nature, that, when applied, makes the successful performance of a job action possible. Knowledge is usually not demonstrated in the action itself but rather by prior education, training, or testing. In observing the action, the knowledge base is assumed and inferred rather than directly observed.

In the above example of the assembler, he or she would need to have sufficient knowledge of the English language to follow directions, know the difference between red and green, and know how to use a screw nut to join the two ends together. The knowledge needed by a surgeon is far more complex and would include an intimate understanding of the anatomy and physiology of the human body, how to monitor the patient's vital signs, choosing the correct scalpel for the procedure, and so on. In both cases, however, each set of knowledge forms the basis of the success of executing the job action.

Skill, the second necessary component for the successful execution of the job action, is defined as the proficiency in the manual, verbal, or mental manipulation of people, ideas, or things. A skill is always directly observable and a certain level of skill is typically set as a standard or baseline for the successful performance of the action.

In our continuing example, the assembler must have sufficient eye-hand coordination to pick up the two ends of the wire and the screw nut and adequate finger dexterity to twist the wires together either by hand or mechanically and insert the twisted ends into the wire nut. The skill set of the surgeon includes a high level of eye-hand coordination, sufficient hand steadiness to manipulate the scalpel without untoward injury to the patient, sufficient finger dexterity to suture major bleeding, and so on. Thus, every job action involves an identification of the required skills and the necessary level of those skills.

Ability is defined as the present capacity to execute a job action, to perform a job function by applying an underlying knowledge base and the necessary skills simultaneously. Knowledge, like ability, is not observable directly but rather is an inferred, higher-order construct, such as problem solving, spatial ability, intelligence, and so on. For lower-level jobs, it is relatively easy to describe the KSA required in terms of just K and S. Abilities are typically invoked in describing higher-level technical, professional, and managerial jobs as the WAs become more conceptual, abstract, and complex, despite the fact that they do not meet the requirements of the Uniform Guidelines of being observable.

Thus, the assembler job could be described readily in terms of the limited knowledge and skill required, while we might invoke such characteristics as systems-orientation, decisiveness, meticulousness, and awareness of the operating room environment as necessary characteristics of a successful surgeon. While most observers would agree that these characteristics are important to surgical success, a number would question whether these characteristics are best understood as abilities.

As a result of such questions, many experts in job analysis (e.g., Harvey, 1991) add a fourth factor, O for Other, to the KSA paradigm, leading to a KSAO approach to job requirements. We believe that both the KSA and the KSAO labels are rather awkward and difficult to apply. Rather, we have chosen to use the term *competencies* as a substitute for these other labels.

We have further proposed an approach (Goodstein & Prien, 2006) in which we separate the technical requirements necessary for job success from the personal/interpersonal requirements. We insist that the more work-related characteristics can and should be included in the job requirements analysis, while the more basic, underlying personality characteristics should be treated separately. Thus, in the case of the surgeon, being systems-oriented and being aware of the OR environment would be regarded as abilities, while being decisive and meticulous would be categorized as more long-standing personal/interpersonal characteristics, ones that would be evidenced more generally in that person's life.

Until recently it was very difficult to identify the personal/interpersonal requirements of job success. The development of the Big Five approach to describing these psychological factors and its widespread adoption, especially in selection, has made this task much easier. The Big Five, also known as the five-factor approach, is based on over a half-century of empirical research that has conclusively shown that five basic factors describe the spectrum of human behavior, and that these characteristics are quite stable over time and are, in various combinations, predictive of on-the-job performance (Barrick & Mount, 1991; Barrick, Mount, & Judge, 2001; Costa, & McCrae, 1992; Digman, 1990).

These five factors are: (1) Neuroticism; (2) Extroversion; (3) Openness to New Experience; (4) Agreeableness; and (5) Conscientiousness, typically abbreviated as NEOAC. Because of the awkwardness of this acronym, we have renamed the five factors as CLUES® — Conscientiousness, Likeableness, Unconventional Thinking, Extroversion, and Stability Goodstein & Lanyon, 2007), an easier label to recall.

For example, it is difficult to think of a successful accountant who is not highly conscientious or a successful sales representative who is not extroverted. Using the Big Five provides job analysts with a uniform vocabulary for describing these intangible but critically important job requirements.

Levels of Job Performance

After developing clarity of the WA involved in a job and the necessary competencies, a job analysis must identify the necessary range of adequate job performance. Most job analyses focus on identifying what constitutes a high level of job performance in order to identify the competencies that separate stars from the rest of the pack. When we are trying to understand these factors to meet promotion or training and development requirements, this is an appropriate approach; but what if we intend to use the job analysis for candidate selection?

Here, a very different dynamic is in play. When we examine the job performance of incumbents, we typically learn what an experienced job holder can accomplish. But few, if any, new hires are likely to be as productive or as competent as the typical incumbent. Thus, in establishing the job performance requirements, we must set more modest initial levels for new hires, a process that requires a fair degree of judgment. One additional point, in selecting supervisors and managers from an existing workforce, it is often the case that a top performer is chosen without recognizing that supervisory and managerial tasks require different skills than performing the tasks being supervised do, so such selections often do not work out satisfactorily. From this discussion it should be clear that job performance levels need to be set as a function of the use to which they are to be put, and that there is no substitute for common sense in setting those limits.

Workplace Characteristics

Workplaces vary enormously in their norms, climate, and culture, in the level of discomfort that workers can experience, the inherent risks posed by working there, and other noteworthy factors. A competent and thorough job analysis identifies the important workplace characteristics. Many approaches to job analyses pay scant attention to describing the workplace setting unless it varies significantly from the typical factory, office, or warehouse. We, on the other hand, strongly believe that an in-depth understanding of the characteristics of the workplace should be an integral part of a competent job analysis. On the basis of this belief, we have included a template for assessing the workplace characteristics as part of this volume in Appendix K.

Once the four elements of the job analysis—the work activities (WA), the job competencies (previously KSAs), the range of job performance, and the workplace characteristics—have been identified, they can be combined in a thematic fashion into a job description. We now turn our attention to the various methods of actually conducting a job analysis.

3

HOW TO CONDUCT A JOB ANALYSIS

The end-product of a job analysis is a job description, a written statement that describes: (1) the important tasks that need to be performed to successfully hold this job; (2) the requirements necessary to perform these tasks; (3) the levels of job performance that can be expected at various levels of experience and expertise; and (4) those characteristics of the work setting that impact work performance. The job description in all cases must be data-based, and clearly the creation of such a document is a time-consuming and labor-intensive process. This chapter provides a road map for creating such a data-based job description.

Methods of Job Analysis

Generally speaking, it is possible to collect data on the first three components of the job analysis simultaneously, while data on the characteristics of the work setting requires a separate, independent assessment. Those doing job analyses should always remember the purpose for which the information is to be used, as this purpose provides the context for both collecting the data and for writing the job description. This is especially true, for example, when collecting job performance data to be used for selection of job applicants. These levels obviously would be different for entry-level or trainee positions than it would be for selecting experienced, high-level operators.

There are five different methods of collecting job analysis data. They are (1) self-reports; (2) direct observations; (3) interviews;

(4) document reviews: and (5) questionnaires and surveys. Each of these is discussed in some detail below. It should be noted that any of these methods can be used either by internal HR staff members or by external consultants with expertise in conducting job analyses who have been engaged for this specific purpose.

Self-Reports

The most obvious and readily available sources of information about a job are the incumbents currently holding that job. All too often, however, incumbent reports are the only source used to analyze a job, because this approach is subject to attempts to inflate the importance of one's job and a variety of other contaminating influences. This is especially the case when incumbents are asked to prepare in writing their own job description with few guidelines and little supervision.

One variation on the self-report approach is to have the job analyst, typically an HR specialist, attempt to fill the job for a brief period and report on his or her experience in filling the job. Obviously, this approach is only appropriate for rather simple jobs that do not require a set of specific skills or much training, and there is always a question of how useful these self-reports are in understanding the job.

Direct Observations

Many jobs can be studied by observing an incumbent actually performing the job. In order to reduce the "audience effect" of having an intrusive observer involved, a video camera can be used to record an incumbent doing the job. Using a camera over a period of time both eliminates the observer effect and provides an opportunity to observe the job over a longer period of time and to take time samples of job behavior from the recording as the database.

Direct observation, however, is most useful with jobs that involve obvious physical activity, activities that are the core of the job. For jobs that are primarily cognitive in nature, direct observation provides little useful data. Observing a market analyst or a theoretical physicist at work would provide us with little information about the nature of their work. Further, neither self-reports nor direct observations provide much information about the requirements necessary to perform these jobs nor about the level of job performance.

Interviews

The limitations of self-report and direct observation have led to the use of interviews as the most widely used approach to job analysis. These interviews must be conducted by a skilled, trained interviewer who has both some understanding of the job being analyzed and the nature of work in general, as these provide the necessary background for asking questions and probing answers for more detailed and complete answers from those being interviewed.

Individual Interviews. There are several sources of information about a job, all of whom can be interviewed, either singly or in small groups. These include current incumbents of the job, supervisors of the job, and others who are often referred to as *subject-matter experts* (SMEs). SMEs are those individuals, other than incumbents, who have knowledge about the job being analyzed, such as former incumbents, managers with oversight of the job, academic specialists, and anyone in the organization who has any specialized knowledge of the job in question. One useful way of identifying SMEs about a particular job is to ask incumbents, "If you're stuck with a job problem that you're having trouble with, who are you most likely to ask for help?" These are the true SMEs, the ones who help those on the job get out of trouble.

In the early, exploratory phase of the job analysis, the initial interviews, which usually should be one-on-one, can be rather unstructured and open-ended as the interviewer starts to learn about the job, the tasks involved, the necessary requirements, and the levels of job performance. As the interviewer gains an understanding of the job and its requirements, he or she should develop an interview protocol that provides a structure for the ensuing interviews, one that enables the interviewer to obtain information about specific aspects of the job under scrutiny and compare the data obtained from different sources.

Group Interviews. These follow-up interviews, usually using the focus group method, are best conducted in a group setting with a mixed group of five or six individuals, incumbents, supervisors, and SMEs. It is imperative that at least two of the group be incumbents—individuals who know the job best—and more than one to ensure surfacing differing points of view. In conducting a focus group, the facilitator should *not* attempt to push for unanimity of viewpoints, but rather should understand that jobs, even what appear to be simple jobs, are seen and performed differently and that these differences need to be woven into the final job description.

The way these group interviews are introduced to the organization, the manner in which individuals are invited to participate, and the way in which the interviews are initiated and conducted are critical to the quality of the information collected. It must be made clear that the purpose of these group interview(s) is to gain a better understanding of a particular job or class of jobs, that no one will lose his or her job as a result of this process, and that what is said in the interview is confidential in that no statement will be attributed to a particular participant. The interviewer must be non-judgmental, listen carefully, play back what was heard, ask questions to clarify points, and take notes on a flip chart in the front of the room.

In conducting these groups, the HR professional should initiate the process with a description of its purpose, together with some discussion about how the results will be used when the process is complete. Next, the group should be prompted to begin discussion of the job or job family to define the tasks involved—the content of the job. It is good practice to have either a flip chart on which this data can be recorded, with the HR professional continuing to probe until the content and structure of the job are adequately addressed. In developing an understanding of the work involved, the interviewer can ask incumbents to describe a typical day, what needs to be done on a regular basis, and what the occasional exceptional requirements are. An alternative approach is to focus attention on either the work flow or organization of individual workers and how their tasks overlap and flow to produce work products. These approaches typically are sufficient to produce a description of the content of the job. The intent here is to generate content while the group has its ideas clearly in mind and then go back and edit that content to conform to acceptable standards.

Having developed an in-depth understanding of the various tasks involved in the job, the next step to identify the necessary requirements to perform the work and then to describe the various levels of job performance. To identify the requirements, the interviewer should ask about what people doing this job need to know and when they need to know it; for example, what tools or equipment are ordinarily used on this job and how skillful does the worker need to be in using them. Further, the interview needs to facilitate the group to identify the requirements for success on this job. Similarly, the group needs to establish in fairly concrete terms the various levels of job performance that can be expected in this job. How many widgets should an expert be able to produce in a typical day, and how many should a relative newcomer to the job be expected to produce. At the end of an interview procedure, the interviewers should feel confident that he or she has gained an understanding of the job being analyzed and can now describe the typical tasks involved in the job, the requirements to perform that job, and the various levels of job performance.

One useful technique to use in the group interview is the *critical incident technique* (Flanagan, 1954) in which the group is asked to describe critical incidents that have occurred on this job that have involved either highly effective or highly ineffective performance. This process has three parts: (1) describe the circumstances in which the job behavior occurred; (2) describe in detail the job behavior itself; and (3) identify the positive or negative consequences of that behavior. These reports of critical incidents often highlight instances of poor judgment, of safety hazards, and of outstanding performance, as well as the role of a variety of personal characteristics on job performance. Inquiring about critical incidents is especially useful when the job seems routine and many of the elements of the job seem obscure to others. Our experience has informed us that SMEs and managers are the most useful sources of critical incident data, which is why including them in these interviews is so important.

Document Reviews

The archives of most organizations contain a variety of documents that are useful in conducting job analyses. These include analyses of output, performance appraisals, reports by both internal auditors and external consultants about workplace issues, and prior job descriptions. Customer complaint records are another highly useful source about employee job behaviors that are of particular importance to customers. Internal memoranda about unusual events, difficulties encountered by workers on a job, or problems in recruiting applicants for a particular job, among many such issues, can provide worthwhile insights into a job. Reports of accidents and medical records are useful in identifying health and safety issues in jobs. Time and attendance records are important sources of information about the importance that workers place on doing that job.

For many years the U.S. military has used a procedure called *after-action reports*, a process for debriefing participants in any important incident to determine what went well and what went poorly, in order to improve future performance in similar situations. The value of such a process in identifying how to improve performance is obvious and thus has been adopted by many non-military organizations as a way to identify issues that need to be addressed in order to improve the organization's performance. The records of such after-action reports, when they exist, are a unique and extraordinary source of information about important elements of job behavior and their impact on organizational outcomes.

Questionnaires and Surveys

Using a job analysis questionnaire can substantially reduce the burden on incumbents and SMEs for developing the information needed for a job analysis. Instead of starting from scratch, those involved in providing information about the job answer a series of questions about the job. The job analyst typically asks the respondents individually to rate the importance of a variety of tasks in the job under scrutiny. The next step is to pick out from a list the requirements necessary to perform, and, finally, to identify the range of job performance using a rating scale. Not only does such a procedure simplify the task for those involved in providing job information, but it also simplifies the job analyst's task of collating and synthesizing the information about the job, easing the task of drafting the job description.

Basically, there are two different approaches to using a job analysis questionnaire. The HR specialist can produce a custom-designed questionnaire especially for this job or he or she can use a commercially available questionnaire.

Custom-Designed Questionnaires. In producing a custom-designed questionnaire, the HR professional responsible for the job analysis must develop the questionnaire using information typically obtained individually from the job incumbent, his or her supervisor, other SMEs, and whatever other data sets are available to the responsible professional. Then small groups of other SMEs make the judgments required by the questionnaire and a computer analyzes the data and provides the necessary descriptions. While using such a custom-designed questionnaire clearly targets the job under investigation, the savings in time and effort of using a questionnaire rather than conducting individual interviews are modest, and a good deal of skill and understanding are required to produce a high-quality custom-designed, job-analysis questionnaire.

Commercially Available Questionnaires. The alternative to a custom-designed job-analysis questionnaire is to use one that has been developed by job-analysis experts and is commercially available. These instruments tend to be well-designed, are fairly reliable, and eliminate the need for an HR professional to develop his or her own instrument. These commercially developed instruments can simply be presented to a group of incumbents and SMEs to complete after providing the group with a relatively straightforward set of instructions about how to proceed. Examples of such questionnaires include the Fleishman Job Analysis Survey (Fleishman, 1996) and the Position Analysis Questionnaire (McCormick, Mehcam, & Jeanneret, 1977.)

This approach, however, tends to have one major disadvantage, namely that the developers of these job-analysis questionnaires have chosen to produce a single questionnaire that covers a wide variety of jobs, from entry-level to managerial. As can well be understood, such a one-size-fits-all approach requires that many of the items are scored as "not part of this job" and so the process of answering the wide range of items required quickly becomes a tedious one, losing the interest of the respondents.

There is an alternative approach, one that we have adopted for this workbook. Our approach provides a set of questionnaires from which the most appropriate one can be selected to analysis a particular job. In Appendices B through I are templates for eight different job-analysis questionnaires, ranging from entry-level jobs involving rather simple tasks and requiring only the most basic requirements to managerial/executive jobs that involve quite complex tasks and requiring a high level of requirements. These eight questionnaires have been developed by us based on our many years of experience in working in a wide range of industries and businesses. Each of these questionnaires is directly based on one or more actual job analyses that we have created with one or more of our client systems.

An HR professional, after a relatively brief study, can select and directly utilize one of these questionnaires to identify the tasks involved in the job and the job requirements for that job, a much less time-consuming and labor-intensive job than developing one from scratch. We need to point out that the use of a job-analysis questionnaire does not obviate the need to augment the information from a questionnaire with data obtained from a discussion of the job with incumbents, observing the job, consulting a variety of records, or doing whatever is possible to develop a fuller understanding of a job and all that it entails.

In summary, in this section we have provided an overview of the various approaches to conducting the critically important HR management tasks of actually doing a job analysis. It should be clear from the above that the process of developing a comprehensive, data-based job analysis is a demanding one, one that requires a high degree of professionalism and competence on the part of the HR professionals who attempt to do job analysis. One of the unfortunate aspects of today's HR management is that this critically important process does not receive the recognition it deserves. We now turn our attention to some of the cautions and caveats that need to be observed in doing job analyses.

Caveats and Cautions

There are a variety of inherent problems in using job descriptions and the underlying job analyses on which these descriptions are based that tend to be overlooked but which, if disregarded, seriously reduce their usefulness. These problems are a function of changes in the nature of work and how work is performed and include changes over time, the low accuracy of the data obtained, and the general stability of job performance.

Changes Over Time

Job descriptions have a half-life, one that varies from job to job, from employer to employer, and from industry to industry. There are a number of reasons for such changes in the way jobs are performed which, in turn, affect the job analysis. One important reason is the ways in which technology has developed and will continue to modify the ways in which work is done. It is difficult for us to think of any job that has not been altered substantially in the past few years as a function of technology. These are not one-time events but are continuous adjustments that reflect the ever-increasing pace of technological advancement.

Jobs change for other reasons, including modifications in supply chain management, the product or service mix offered by the organization, customer requirements, and so on. Some of these changes are by-products of technological change and others are not. But regardless of their origin, such changes mean that job descriptions rapidly become out-of-date and require a new job analysis to make them current.

Low Accuracy

There is ample evidence to support the conclusion that the ratings that constitute the core of any job analysis are less than reliable (e.g., Hughes & Prien, 1989). Incumbents and supervisors may not provide valid ratings and other data about the nature of the job. They may attempt to inflate (or deflate) the importance of the job or of elements of the job, and they often have quite different experience of the job under review. Furthermore, data may be distorted for personal or political reasons, for example, over-emphasizing the similarity of this job to other jobs, rather than its uniqueness. Or the job may not be being performed adequately or may be misunderstood, and so on.

These factors, among others, simply mean that a competent job analysis must involve multiple raters with a range of backgrounds and experience. The HR professional conducting the job analysis should closely examine the data, particularly the ratings on job analysis inventories, for gross differences and follow up with individual discussions to resolve these differences. Here is yet another reason for professionalism on the part of those engaged in job analysis.

Lack of Stability

Finally, in many jobs there is an inherent instability in the work performed, such as those jobs that have a seasonal variation in the tasks involved. In the most obvious example, farmers regularly go through the cycle of preparing the fields, planting, fertilizing and weeding, and harvesting. A competent job analysis must involve the entire cycle. But such seasonality influences other jobs as well. The work of accountants is intensified during the tax preparation season, as is that of retail-store clerks during the Christmas rush. Those engaged in conducting job analyses need to be aware of such seasonal trends and factor these in when planning their data collection.

Another reason for the lack of stability of jobs is the tendency over time of incumbents to *improve* the ways in which tasks are performed, whether or not such improvements are known to supervisors and managers, or even if these modifications really improve either the process or the product. If a job analysis is not current, such changes in how work is accomplished will not be part of the job description.

In this section we have focused on why job analyses and job descriptions may not be as accurate as expected. These concerns simply highlight the need for keeping job descriptions very current and for having competent HR professionals conduct job analyses. We now turn our attention to our eight job analysis templates, their development, and how they should be used.

4

THE JOB ANALYSIS TEMPLATES

We have long been interested in the nature of work, of what various jobs entail, the characteristics required for success on jobs, and how these factors interact with the characteristics of the workplace. These interests have facilitated our careers as consultants to a broad range of organizations, ranging from small, start-up operations to massive, global conglomerates. Our experience includes a variety of organizations in the United States, Europe, and Asia, including manufacturing and service businesses; municipal, state, and federal government agencies; and nonprofit organizations of all types.

The Development of the Templates

One recurring theme of our work with organizations has been in developing and improving their procedures, both for conducting job analyses and for linking these job analyses to a variety of human capital applications. We estimate that, over our years of professional practice and research, we and our associates have conducted job analysis studies for over five thousand different jobs. While we readily admit that there is a large degree of overlap among these many jobs, we nevertheless believe that this experience has given us an in-depth understanding of the nature of work and how it is organized in jobs, job families, and careers.

On the basis of these experiences, we have developed a series of eight templates, each for a different job or family of jobs. That is, we have created eight different, generic job descriptions that can be used as the starting point in developing the analysis of a specific job. This approach, in contrast to the *one-size-fits-all* approach of most other available job analysis templates, allows for beginning the process with a more restricted and better targeted set of questions, ones aimed at the *job family* in which the job to be studied readily fits. A job family is simply a group of jobs involving more-or-less the same tasks and similar competencies.

We faced a dilemma in determining how many templates to develop. On the one hand, we wanted enough templates to cover the many thousands of job titles that exist in our economy, while on the other hand, too many templates would be unwieldy and choosing among them might be problematic. On the basis of both our experience and some field testing, we distilled the many jobs into eight general job families and developed a template for each of these.

Thus, rather than starting with a questionnaire intended to cover all jobs in the workplace, our approach narrows the field to questions that we know are by and large appropriate for most jobs in that job family. For example, to begin an analysis the job for a file clerk, we would begin by selecting the Clerical template, where all of the questions are directly concerned with clerical and minor administrative tasks, rather than dealing with a variety of job tasks that clearly do not fit into that rubric.

We recognize that, in some cases, it may be difficult to decide which template is appropriate to use. However, our experience has shown that it is easier to choose a more-or-less appropriate template and edit that, rather than begin the process from scratch. While it may take some time to edit the template chosen, the editing time and effort will be quite different from that involved when using a single-purpose generic model. Further, the fact that these templates can be downloaded from a website simplifies such editing.

Eight Templates for Job Analysis

The eight job family templates, arranged in order of complexity, are as follows with the appendix in which each can be found in parentheses:

- Entry Level (Appendix B)
- Production/Operations (Appendix C)
- Clerical (Appendix D)
- Sales and Sales Management (Appendix E)
- Clerical/Administrative Services (Appendix F)
- Professional Administrative (Appendix G)
- Supervisory/First-Line Manager (Appendix H)
- Senior Management/Executive (Appendix I)

Each template includes two parts, the first of which provides the rater with a list of *work activities* (WA). Each WA is to be rated as to how important this WA is in doing this job, with a rating of "0" indicating that this activity is not involved in this particular job while a rating of "5" indicates that this WA is one of the most essential activities performed on this job.

The second part of the template is concerned with the *competencies* necessary to be successful on these jobs. In the preceding chapter we pointed out that we will be using the term *competencies* instead of the earlier KSAO rubric. This consists of rating a variety of job-related competencies on how important each is for doing this job, with a rating of "0" indicating that this is *not* a requirement for doing the this job while a rating of "5" indicates that this requirement is one of the most essential to being fully effective in doing this job.

Let us now turn to a brief description of each of these templates and the types of jobs that typically can the studied by applying that template.

Entry-Level Job Analysis Template (Appendix B)

These generic entry-level jobs are typically considered *an extra pair of hands*, the skill requirements are minimal, and the jobs are menial. Job titles at this level include, for example, laborer, janitor, security guard, materials handler, and loader. In the skilled trades, these workers are seen as helpers to electricians, plumbers, and the like, while service jobs include such titles as orderly, valet parker, dishwasher, and maintenance worker. These jobs typically require an ability to follow directions, the willingness to exert effort, and a conscientious nature. In industrial settings, some degree of physical strength or agility often is also required. Typically, no specific level of education is required and the training time is minimal. While at one time these jobs did not require literacy, it is now expected, at least implicitly.

Production Operations Job Analysis Template (Appendix C)

Production operators are found in virtually all light-industrial settings and in many heavy industries. Included are such jobs as assemblers, machine operators, quality-control inspectors, and the like. These jobs require both a level of literacy and a higher level of knowledge and skill than those at the entry level. The tasks may include reading gauges, adjusting machinery and equipment, reading diagrams, instruments, manuals, and the like, planning and organizing work, and so on. A high school diploma, trade school certificate, or the equivalent is usually the minimum requirement for these jobs, and there can be fairly extensive training involved. Hiring for these jobs can be quite selective and there is considerable variety in the tasks in this job family.

Clerical Job Analysis Template (Appendix D)

In contrast to the production operations, these jobs are performed in an office setting rather than an industrial one, although many such jobs exist in factories. The emphasis in such jobs is primarily on mental rather than physical activities, although some slight physical activities may be involved. Among the tasks involved in this job family are filing and retrieving records, transcribing reports and letters, basic formatting and editing of written documents, scheduling, computing and verifying data, preparing reports, and so on. Job titles include file clerk, call center representative, transcriber, data entry clerk, and so on. These jobs involve a wide range of tasks and often require independent functioning. They usually require a high school diploma or the equivalent, and some on-the-job training may be involved. Finally, there is an ever-increasing emphasis on interpersonal skills, since such work often requires collaboration with others.

Sales and Sales Management Job Analysis Template (Appendix E)

Success in sales is far more a function of the individual's personal/interpersonal skills than of any technical know-how. One exception is technical sales, where product knowledge often requires some in-depth understanding of scientific and technical data. Beyond this important exception, the many types of sales jobs involve other differences, for example, between inside and outside sales, between selling tangibles (goods) and intangibles (services), so the WA analysis should identify the tasks involved and the requirements.

We have included sales management in this template rather than in the Senior Management/Executive Job Analysis Template, as sales personnel are often required to fulfill some sales management responsibilities and sales managers are almost always drawn from the ranks of the sales force. Thus the work activities and the competencies involved in sales management have much in common with those of sales personnel. For high-level sales management jobs, it may be necessary to combine this template with the Senior Management/Executive Job Analysis Template to fully describe both the Work Activities and the necessary Competencies.

Most retail sales jobs, on the other hand, ordinarily should be evaluated by using the clerical template, as there is little actually selling involved. The job titles always include the word "sales" and we typically include customer-service representative in this category, especially when they have problem-solving authority. For higher-level sales positions, a college degree is usually required and some on-the-job training is typical.

Clerical/Administrative Services Job Analysis Template (Appendix F)

Professional and technical service jobs include such jobs as senior technical consultant, graphic designer, professional writer or editor, systems engineer, marketing specialist, senior programmer, and so on. Given the wide variety of these jobs, producing a single generic template that will fit all is more difficult than for any of the other job families. Therefore, to provide a suitable model our template emphasizes technical jobs in information systems. This example should serve as a useful tool for customizing other jobs in this wide-ranging job family. Moreover, many high-level professional jobs such as physician, attorney, research scientist, and the like are so unique and specialized that none of our templates fit. This means that, beyond a very basic level of description, this template may be of limited use and conventional HR procedures may not be useful or applicable. Invariably, these jobs require a college and frequently an advanced degree.

Professional Administrative Job Analysis Template (Appendix G)

In contrast to the Clerical Job Analysis Template, here we are concerned with high-level administrative tasks, such as schedul-ing meetings, interacting with senior executives, arranging travel, coordinating work flow, and managing office procedures. While there may be some supervisory responsibilities, usually of other office workers, this is not a supervisory position. Job titles include administrative assistant, administrative specialist, staff assistant, executive assistant, and office manager. These jobs invariably require a high degree of tact and good judgment, and often some technical skills are required, such as budgeting, applying software, and managing travel. These jobs usually require a college degree, although experience can often be substituted.

Supervisory/First-Line Manager Job Analysis Template (Appendix H)

These jobs all involve the direct supervision of other employees, including giving directions, setting priorities, scheduling, securing the required resources for task completion, and providing guidance, coaching, and performance feedback. Conflict resolution and problem solving are import areas for these jobs. Job titles include foreperson, supervisor, and manager. These jobs require good communication skills, a good deal of interpersonal sensitivity, and a willingness to confront difficult situations. The model template presented emphasizes manufacturing/industrial jobs. Therefore, using it for jobs in other settings, such as in services organizations, will require some modification of the specific activities and competencies. A college degree is usually preferred, although years of experience in similar organizations often can be a substitute.

Senior Management/Executive Job Analysis Template (Appendix I)

At the top of the occupational pyramid are the management and executive jobs. Jobs at this level typically involve abstract and conceptual thinking and require the incumbent to consider the impact of decisions over an extended time frame. A high level of communication skills, strategic thinking, a good grasp of finances, and superior interpersonal skills are usually necessary. Job titles include president, chief executive officer, managing director, chief financial officer, vice president of marketing, and the like. A minimum of a college degree is usually required and advanced degrees, such as an MBA, are often preferred. Prior experience in a related industry at a senior level is usually expected.

Using the Templates

These instructions are intended to take the user through the sequence of steps involved in the proper use of the templates.

1. Clearly identify the job that you wish to analyze. Learn as much as you can about that job by observing people in the job, interviewing incumbents, reading existing job descriptions, surfing the web for information, and checking out what your colleagues know about this job.

2. On the basis of your knowledge of the job, review the eight templates and select the template that is the best fit for that job.

3. With the target job in mind, review the general instructions for that template and both the sets of activities and the competencies. Feel free to edit either or both of the data sets to ease the task that you are about to assign.

4. Identify the several raters whom you will ask to complete the template for this job. Those you invite to be raters should be *subject-matter experts*, that is, they should have recent, extensive knowledge of the job. These could be incumbents, supervisors, managers, or external experts. When requesting their assistance in completing this task you should stress the importance to you of this work, explain how it is to be used, and work collaboratively to set a certain date for completing the task.

5. It is important to stress to each of these experts the need for a careful, thorough, and systematic approach to completing the template. Remember the old adage, "Garbage in, garbage out!" Following agreement to complete a template, it is usually appropriate to send an email or a note of appreciation to each expert rater for accepting this responsibility and a reminder of the agreed-on date for completion.

6. When you receive the completed template, you should review the data for completeness and for any suggestion that the task was not taken seriously. Indications of this include using the same response throughout the template, responding randomly or regularly using a pattern, such as "1," "2," "3," "4," and "5." Do not assume that each expert responded professionally, even though this is what you would hope for. Any template that has indications of lack of commitment or carelessness should be discarded. This is one of the reasons why you need multiple raters.

7. Once you have assured yourself that you have done your quality control and that you have a sufficient number of valid ratings, then you can move on to enter the data into the template summary spreadsheets and calculate your results. At this point you are halfway home.

8. We typically use an rating of "3" or greater to define initially both the WA and the competencies. After identifying those items with such ratings, you need to review the actual items and determine whether they meet a test of reasonableness. One of the reasons that you initially invested your time and effort is to develop sufficient understanding of the job to make such judgments. Among the questions you might ask are: Did I select the right template? Did the SME seem to do a competent job? Are there any reasons to be skeptical about these results? If the data seem logical and reasonable, you move to the next step.

9. The next step, the final review, involves completing the Summary of Importance of Work Activities and Competencies that is provided as Appendix J.

After reviewing these procedures, if you feel that you need a more in-depth understanding of this process, we recommend that you do a trial run, using one of the less complex jobs—a job with which you are familiar.

Completing the Summary Forms

The form below provides a convenient way to summarize the importance that selected raters give to the various work activities and to the related competencies. The detailed instructions for using these forms are provided in Appendix J and we have reproduced these instructions below and provided a sample of a partially completed Work Activity Importance Ratings form to illustrate its use.

Summary of Work Activity Importance Ratings

Target Job Title:_____

Location:_____ Date:_____

This form provides a convenient way to summarize the ratings of the importance of the various work activities that have been identified by the selected raters as important on this particular job. In rating the importance of each work activity, the raters used the following rating scale:

Rating Meaning of the Rating

0   This rating indicates that the work activity is never done and is not part of the job.

1   This rating indicates that the work activity has only minor importance relative to other activities performed by individuals in this job. Considering all activities, it would have the lowest priority or importance.

2   This rating indicates that the work activity has a relatively low level of importance compared to other job activities.

3   This rating indicates that the work activity is moderately important for fully effective job performance relative to other activities, and has about average priority among all activities performed.

4   This rating indicates that the work activity is very important to fully effective job performance. It has a higher degree of importance or priority than most other activities.

Ordinarily we are concerned only with importance ratings of "3" or higher. Any rating lower than "3" is unlikely to be an important descriptor of the job and can be safely ignored. Therefore we have provided summary forms for only the top three ratings—3, 4, and 5.

Each of the forms in Appendix J contains a column for each item in the template, plus columns for recording each rater's assessment of that item. For example, using the summary form for Work Activities rated "5," the person completing the summary should simply go through the template completed by the first rater and place a check mark in the box for every item that received a "5" rating—one that indicated that this Work Activity was essential to performing this job. The summarizer should then do the same for those items rated "4" and then "3," using the appropriate summary form. The summary forms provided list

Sample Completed Form: Essential Work Activities Rated 5

Item	Raters								
	1	2	3	4	5	6	7	8	9
1	✓			✓					N/A
2							✓	✓	
3									
4	✓	✓	✓	✓	✓	✓	✓	✓	
5				✓	✓				
6		✓	✓	✓	✓	✓	✓	✓	
7	✓								
8									
9									
10		✓				✓			
11									
12				✓		✓		✓	
13									
14	✓	✓			✓				
15	✓		✓			✓			
16									
17									
18				✓		✓			
19	✓	✓	✓		✓	✓	✓	✓	

the maximum number of items that can be rated in any of the standard templates. If any additional items have been added or more than eight raters are involved, additional copies of these forms can be duplicated.

After the Work Activities ratings are entered on the three summary forms, a similar process should be used to enter the competency ratings, using the provided summary forms. These ratings of both the work activities and job competencies can then be used in the writing of the job description.

In this sample, you will notice that each rater judged only four to six of the nineteen activities reported as essential. They were unanimous only on Item 4, and nearly unanimous on Items 6 and 19, so these three items should be regarded as essential to doing this job. Eight other work activities received two or three ratings of "5," one activity received one 5, and seven items received none. When summaries of the ratings of "4" and "3" are completed, it will be important to note whether any of the eight receiving two or three ratings of "5" received a significant number of these ratings, which would suggest that they may indeed be either essential or extremely important to performing this job. Moreover, any activities or competencies judged "4" or "5" by at least half the raters should be highlighted in the final job description.

Once you have completed your summary analysis of the work activities and competencies, it is time to turn your attention to determining the workplace characteristics that affect this job using the Workplace Characteristics Profile in Appendix K.

5

THE WORKPLACE CHARACTERISTICS PROFILE

While the work activities and the competencies necessary to perform these activities are critical elements in defining a job, no job is performed in a vacuum. Every job is performed in a workplace and thus the characteristics of that workplace are critical elements to be identified in defining and understanding that job. In the most obvious examples, workplaces that pose a clear danger to workers—such as police, fire fighting, and the military—or that involve dealing with hazardous or toxic materials are workplace characteristics that are of great importance in defining those jobs. But every workplace has important characteristics that need to be identified and quantified in a job analysis.

While workplace danger or the handling of hazardous materials have clear impact on how work is done, many other workplace conditions that impact work and workers. These include long hours, shift work, toxic managers, harassment for any number of reasons, job insecurity, and the fear of downsizing, to mention just a few. While the importance of most of these more obvious negative workplace characteristics should be clear to anyone doing a job analysis, it is less clear how to define and assess the more subtle workplace characteristics that also can have a significant impact on workers.

Organizational Culture and Climate

While industrial/organizational psychologists have long been interested in understanding the nature of the workplace, they have tended to focus on defining and understanding the *culture* of the organization as a way of understanding human systems and how they operate. Typically, definitions of organizational culture are based on an "open systems" approach to organizations where each aspect of an organization's culture interacts with some or all of the other aspects to guide organizational behavior. The Burke-Litwin model is but one example of such an open-systems model (Burke, 2002).

Organizational Culture

Since no single, universally accepted definition of organizational culture exists, our definition attempts to capture the principal elements of most popular definitions. We define organizational culture as the pattern of shared basic assumptions that an organization has developed as it has addressed and resolved issues in its dealings with the external environment and its internal operations. As organizations develop over time, these assumptions are tested and those that continue to help the organization thrive coalesce into a culture, one that is taught to new members as the right way to perceive, think about, and resolve these external and internal issues.

Among the several authors who have provided definitions of organizational culture and provided models of such cultures are Deal and Kennedy (2000), Burke (2002), Schein (2004), Hofstede and Hofstede (2005), and Morgan (2006), among others. Because the Hofstede and Hofstede model is both the most comprehensive and the only one based on a large database, it is useful as an illustration of such models. Their model involves five dimensions:

- Power distance—the degree of hierarchy and lack of equality in the distribution of power
- Uncertainty avoidance—degree of comfort or discomfort with uncertainty and lack of structure
- Individualism—focus on individualism on the one hand versus collectivity on the other

- Masculinity versus femininity—toughness versus tenderness
- Long-term versus short-term orientation—focus on long-term versus short-term goals and payoffs

While such models of organizational culture are useful tools for describing and understanding organizations on a conceptual level, especially at the executive and managerial level and how strategy and decision making occur at that level, such models lack the comprehensiveness and specificity to describe the workplace as it is experienced by rank-and-file employees.

Organizational Climate

Although organizational culture is generally seen as deep, stable, and organization-wide; organizational climate, on the other hand, according to Burke (1993) is "the collective impressions, expectations, and feelings of the members of local work units" (p. 131). Burke goes on to point out that, in his view, organization climate changes day-to-day as a function of the many transactions in which the work unit engages, both internally and between the work unit and the rest of the organization as well as with the external environment. This suggests that the workplace characteristics that are part of most job descriptions are not simply a matter of organizational culture.

While there is general agreement in the professional literature that both organizational climate and organization culture are important aspects in understanding how organizations function, there is less agreement about how to define and measure each of these aspects, especially organizational climate. Moreover, the various instruments that are available to measure both organizational culture and climate appear to have rather different foci, as suggested by their different approaches and content. On the basis of these considerations, we concluded that, for the purposes of this book, we needed to develop a measure of workplace characteristics, one that was useful to persons conducting job analyses.

The Workplace Characteristics Profile

We begin by defining workplace characteristics as those relatively stable characteristics of workplaces that impact—positively or negatively—the manner in which work is done. In developing our Profile, we decided not to include those special workplace characteristics that set a workplace clearly apart from workplaces in general, that is, high risk, danger, the handling of toxic or hazardous material, or other features of the workplace that are not present in the overwhelming majority of jobs. Obviously, we do not mean to underplay the importance of such workplace characteristics, but we believe that they are so obvious on the one hand, and so unusual on the other, that including them would simply overcomplicate the task of describing the characteristics of most workplaces.

Developing the WCP

We decided to base the Workplace Characteristic Profile (WCP) on some of our earlier research in this area (Prien, 1989). In developing that earlier version, then called the Work Setting Characteristics Inventory, we did an initial, careful review of the research literature that identified a large number of factors that had been used to characterize workplaces. From this long list of characteristics, we were able to develop a preliminary taxonomy, essentially based on recurring elements usually included in organizational self-descriptions. The following fourteen dimensions emerged from this sorting process:

1. Conformity and propriety
2. Responsibility
3. Feedback and reward
4. Task identity
5. Effectiveness
6. Managing change

7. Crisis management

8. Communication

9. Formalized job roles

10. Standardization of tasks

11. Role specialization

12. Management control

13. Centralization of authority

14. Technology

This taxonomy served as the basis for developing the initial version of the new Workplace Characteristics Profile (WCP). Using a variety of different sources, including our earlier literature review, fifty-six items were developed, four for each of the fourteen dimensions. Each item was written to tap a different facet of that dimension to produce a comprehensive inventory.

As we have detailed in our earlier research report (Prien, 1989), the WCP was used in a series of three separate studies, each involving over one hundred individuals in sales/marketing, finance/accounting, and manufacturing organizations, to determine the factorial structure of the instrument and to eliminate any items that did not fit that structure. On the basis of this research, the WCP was reduced to a thirty-five-item inventory that tapped seven major, relatively independent dimensions. Each scale was comprised of five items. The scales were

1. *Efficiency*—Focus on being productive continually;

2. *Communication*—Emphasis on communicating with others, especially to seek job-related information;

3. *Standardization of roles*—Emphasis on standardized work roles and on following the established rules;

4. *Task standardization*—Focus on performing job tasks in a prescribed, standard fashion;

5. *Change management*—Focus on effectiveness in dealing with changes required by the external environment;

6. *Specialization of role*—Emphasis on becoming expert on one's job and following the chain of command; and

7. *Independence of action*—Focus on exercising initiative and making a contribution.

These initial seven factor-based scales have been shown to be useful indices on how organizations are perceived by those working there. Further, these scales have been shown (Prien, 1989) to be valid indicators of changes in those perceptions as a function of a variety of organizational development (OD) interventions, including the introduction of an extensive training and development program, the implementation of a total quality management program, and a supervisory training program. But their major use has proven to be as part of the job analysis process.

Continuing use of the WCP has led us to make adjustments to match the major changes in important characteristics of the workplace. Our informal research has led us to include five additional factors to the original seven, making twelve in all. Four of the five new scales address the dramatic increase in workforce diversity:

8. *Accommodating to persons with disabilities*—Focus on facilitating the entry and success of persons with disabilities in the workplace;

9. *Accommodating to persons from diverse backgrounds*—Focus on integrating persons not from mainstream backgrounds;

10. *Promoting gender equality*—Emphasis providing equal treatment for men and women throughout the workplace; and

11. *Controlling harassment*—Focus is on actively discouraging harassment of others for any reason.

These four factors are not only an important aspect of current HR management, but they are also necessary as an important way of reducing the risk of litigation for violations of the many federal, state, and local laws outlawing such workplace behavior. These four new scales reflect the implications of workforce changes. But the workforce is not the only element that is changing. Virtually everything is changing. Hence, we have added a fifth new scale:

12. *Managing change*—Focus is on providing information about change and support in managing change.

We have identified this new, twelve-factor scale as the Workplace Characteristics Profile, a copy of which can be found in Appendix K.

Administering the WCP

The WCP should be used to identify those characteristics of the workplace that can either help or hinder most employees from successfully doing their jobs. The WCP should be completed by a cross-section of persons who have had the opportunity to experience this workplace and who can be expected to provide a valid picture of that workplace. At least six to eight persons at various levels of the organization should complete the WCP, and their responses should be used to create a mean profile, one that highlights the major issues that a worker must contend with on a regular basis.

Additionally, any unusual workplace characteristic that merit inclusion, such as physical risk or any of the others mentioned above, should be identified by interviewing each individual who completed the WCP. The mean profile and the interview data thus become the basis for describing the important characteristics of the workplace in the final job description.

Interpreting the WCP

Each of the twelve scales of the WCP can be further understood based on the nature of the items that comprise the scales, which are summarized below and also described in Appendix K.

Managing Work Efficiently. Emphasis is on the efficient management of work in an increasingly dynamic and complex environment. Effectiveness of work performed is evidenced by the quality and quantity of output, and individuals are expected to adapt and orchestrate their activities on a relatively continuous basis in order to maintain efficiency. High scores on this factor indicate a strong focus on efficiency throughout the workplace.

Accommodating to Persons with Disabilities. Emphasis is on accommodating persons with disabilities. There is a focus on assisting individuals to overcome limitations and on facilitating individuals' efforts to overcome workplace obstacles. High scores indicate a focus on what individuals can do, how they can do it, and the adaptations and accommodations required by others for effective workplace functioning.

Communicating with Others. Emphasis is on communicating with others and seeking job-related information to increase both efficiency and effectiveness. Such information may come from a variety of sources—the work or work products, formal or informal contact—and is generally easily accessible. High scores indicate that individuals are expected to coordinate and communicate with others in order to obtain information for improving the quality and quantity of output.

Accommodating to Persons from Different Backgrounds. The emphasis is on adapting to people who do not come from the mainstream, but rather from the evolving heterogeneity of the workplace. Such persons come from different cultures and are different in their appearance, dress, attitudes, speech, and so on, and they often need acceptance and support to be successful in the workplace. High scores on this factor indicate a commitment to providing such acceptance and support.

Standardization of Work Roles and Procedures. Emphasis is on standardization of work roles and procedures. It exemplifies the classical bureaucratic characteristic of role standardization in which individuals know what they should do and know what is expected of them, and thus produce a continuity of activities. Individuals can predict accurately what is going to happen and how they are expected to react. High scores on this factor suggest a commitment to a bureaucratic approach to management.

Promoting Gender Equality. Emphasis is on providing equal treatment of men and women in the workplace—in job assignments, promotional opportunities, access to training, equality in pay and benefits, and all other important aspects of work. High scores on this factor indicate that there is clear support by management for a zero-tolerance policy of discrimination on the basis of gender.

Standardizing Tasks and Performance. Emphasis is on standardizing tasks and standardized performance of these job tasks. High scores on this factor indicate that tasks must be performed in a specified manner and that standardized approaches are required. High scores indicate that these are significant characteristics of the workplace and the individual has little discretion about managing his or her performance.

Managing Change. Emphasis is on providing support for employees in understanding the need for change, in coping with change, and in embarking on the many transitions required by changing conditions in the workplace. High scores indicate a generalized understanding that the environment is in a state of constant flux and that everyone needs to be prepared to adapt to these changes.

Managing Work for Effectiveness. Emphasis is on responding effectively to external forces. This approach is characterized by a focus on responding promptly to market changes, including customer wants and needs, other market shifts, competition, changing technology, laws and regulations. High scores on this scale suggest that persons are empowered to act without precedent and without guidance from others.

Controlling Harassment. Emphasis is on active discouragement of workplace harassment, intentional or unintentional, harassment based on race, age, gender, sexual orientation, physical limitation, or religion. There is clear support by management of a zero-tolerance policy against any form of workplace harassment.

Promoting Specialization. Emphasis is on developing and using a specialized skill that is regularly used on the job. This promotion of specialization precludes members of a work group from being cross-trained or alternating task assignments. High scores indicate that this bureaucratic approach prevents taking independent action to solve problems.

Promoting Independence of Action. Emphasis is on exercising independence of action. Individuals are expected to perform relatively independently and are held accountable through meeting output expectations and maintaining a high level of expertise. High scores indicate that individuals are encouraged to exercise initiative and take risks.

Finally, having identified the important workplace characteristics, we turn our attention to the procedures for establishing the various levels of job performance in our final chapter.

6

ESTABLISHING JOB PERFORMANCE LEVELS

A comprehensive job analysis consists of three components: (a) the specific competencies required for successful job performance; (b) the important characteristics of the workplace that might impact job performance; and (c) the level of job performance required for success. The focus of this chapter is on identifying and specifying the processes involved in determining the specific level of job performance required for a given job.

It is important to recognize that the measurement of job performance is one of the most vexing problems in the management of human resources. It is a complex issue because performance can be measured in so many different ways. There the standard or set of final criteria against which any performance measure can be compared must include consideration of the purpose for the application. At the same time, the issue of measuring job performance is critical, as it underlies virtually all HR decisions from recruitment, to hiring, promotion, compensation, and retention.

Competencies and Jobs

The first thing to recognize when establishing performance levels of a job is that different competencies relate to effective performance of many different jobs. The requirements for success may vary widely depending on the requirements of a specific job. Two such competencies are oral communication and problem solving. The high-level jobs heavily dependent on high levels of oral communication competency are easy to reel off—executives in large organizations, attorneys, and journalists, to name but a few. Other high-level jobs, such as research scientists or novelists, may have only modest needs for this competency. At the opposite end of the labor market similar differences exist. Receptionists and call center staff are examples of jobs requiring strong oral communication competency. Most basic labor jobs, whether in construction sites, factory floors, or agricultural fields, do not need workers with this competency.

Problem-solving competency presents a similar picture. This competency is central to the work of both research scientists and most technical-service representatives, while it is not needed by food preparation workers, word processors, and/or typists.

In establishing performance levels we are concerned with the levels within a specific job in a specific organization, not with differences in performance levels between jobs. Determining the minimal level of acceptable job performance, the range of expected performance, and what constitutes truly superior performance is a critical part of any job analysis. While we are primarily concerned with establishing job performance levels as part of conducting a job analysis, we should note that there are several other important uses of data on job performance.

The Uses of Job Performance Data

Among the several uses of job performance data are in (a) recruitment, (b) creating career ladders, (c) evaluating organizational performance, and (d) improving organizational performance. Let us briefly examine each of these in turn.

Recruitment

As we noted earlier in Chapter 2, the performance data obtained as part of the job analysis play a critical role in any recruitment effort. These performance data help establish the level of each competency being sought. But this is not a straightforward process. When there is high unemployment and thus a large applicant pool, setting high performance standards is an appropriate strategy. On the other hand, when a tight labor market yields a small pool of applicants, setting a lower level of minimum performance is often necessary in order to secure an adequate pool of applicants. Knowing the range of the acceptable level of the required job competencies is essential for making these assumptions.

Creating Career Ladders

When an organization must hire individuals below the optimal level of a critical job competency, establishing a career ladder is crucial. A *career ladder* consists of a series of steps from the lowest acceptable level of competence at which an employee can be hired up to what is typically referred to as the full-performance level. Such a career ladder enables an employee to pass through a progression of increasing responsibility linked to some acknowledgement or recognition.

The establishment of such career ladders has many benefits for both employees and the organization. Career ladders broaden the pool of applicants and provide greater flexibility in hiring. They may also enhance employee job satisfaction and employee motivation and thus increase job retention. Providing internal job opportunities and reducing the cost of acquiring human capital is another advantage.

However, once career ladders are established it is incumbent on the employer to ensure that such ladders truly enable employees to advance upward. This typically involves making available any necessary training and development programs. The company must also provide employees with assignments of increasing difficulty, and provide the mentoring and coaching necessary to ensure satisfactory job performance. What is critical to this situation is clearly understood, definitive information about job performance.

Evaluating Organizational Performance

Organizations, especially high-performing ones, regard performance data as empirical information about the quality of the operations and how well they are meeting their customer or stakeholder requirements. Whether applied over the longer term or for short-term corrective actions, performance information is required for the evaluation and used as an underpinning for the continuous improvement of overall management and strategic planning processes.

Specifically, job performance data provides various levels of management and employees with performance information. These data enable them to determine when corrective action is necessary and when changes are necessary, in the performance measurement system. When it is clear that changes in the organization's actual level of job performance are required, an organization must then develop an action plan for improving that performance.

Improving Organizational Performance

Reasons for low levels of job performance are many and complex. Paramount issues include employee limitations, poor supervision, lack of appropriate training and development, inadequate recognition and reward systems, organizational structural issues, poor internal communication, and organizational culture, to name but a few of the more obvious ones. Once it is determined that job performance is placing the organization in a non-competitive position, the organization should move swiftly to identify and address the underlying reasons for this problem. Obviously, accurate and dependable job performance data are necessary for any of this to occur.

Methods for Measuring Job Performance

In general there are two approaches to measuring job performance —objective and subjective. An *objective measure* is based directly on quantitative performance assessments, while subjective measures involve the judgment of an external observer, presumably on the basis of first-hand data.

Objective Measures

In virtually all organizations, objective data on individual performance are available, even if not regularly collated, analyzed, and used. Specific measures depend on the nature of the business and include such data points as dollar value of sales, key strokes or words per minute, number of customer minutes on hold, amount of rework, or number of errors over a specified period of time. Other objective measures include number of days tardy or absent, job longevity, accidents, and other indices of performance.

Given the easy availability of such data, the question arises as to why these measures are not used more often as indices of performance. While clearly some, such as accidents, rework, tardiness, and absences, are used regularly, most are not. A variety of reasons explain why. Let us use the example of objective measures of sales performance to highlight at least two of the major problems that arise when using such measures. These problems are deficient criterion measures and unequal opportunities.

When we use the dollar value of sales as *the* criterion of success, we ignore other critical elements involved in successful sales, such as customer satisfaction, reorders, and so on. Thus, in most cases, relying on the dollar value of sales is an example of a *deficient criterion measure*.

Further, the dollar value of sales is a function of factors other than the actions of the sales person. These other factors beyond the control of the employee may include the size or spread of the territory, the quality of available leads, the nature of the customer base, and so on. These *unequal opportunity* factors reduce the utility of the sales volume as the sole criterion of success. It would be easy to find other examples, but we believe that we have made our point: objective measures are not all that they have been cracked up to be. Although these objective measures, collated over an entire organization, are highly useful for comparisons with competitors or changes over time, they are of limited use for understanding individual job performance. The major inherent problem with using a single objective measure of performance is that it cannot take into account the complexity of factors that impact an employee's job performance.

Subjective Measures

Typical solutions to this problem rely on using rating scales that allow one or more external observers to report their observations of an individual's job performance in one or more measures. Since these ratings involve the judgment of the observer(s), they are regarded as *subjective measures*.

Over time a variety of different rating scales have been developed for evaluating individual job performance. The most commonly used form is the *graphic rating scale*, an example of which is shown in Figure 6.1.

As can be seen in Figure 6.1, the form asks the rater to evaluate the quality of the individual's work along a continuum from low to high, using a five-point scale. Such rating scales often provide a definition of the performance characteristic to

Figure 6.1 A Simple Graphic Rating Scale

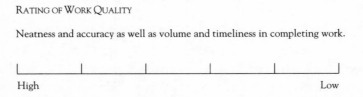

RATING OF WORK QUALITY

Neatness and accuracy as well as volume and timeliness in completing work.

High   Low be evaluated. For example, in rating the quality of work for an office assistant, work quality might be defined as "Neatness and accuracy as well as volume and timeliness in completing work." This type of graphic rating scale is of limited usefulness because it provides only quantitative end points that are not well defined, even with the description provided.

Figure 6.2 presents another version of a graphic rating scale that attempts to provide more specific verbal anchors for the two end-points and the middle, as well as numerical anchors, is an improvement over the one in Figure 6.1. However, the lack of adequate behavioral definitions of the various levels of performance remains a limitation. Raters may have very different notions of what constitutes competent performance and, therefore, of what constitutes greater or less than competent performance. Consequently, their ratings depend to a large extent on personal values, breadth of experience, and so on.

An example of arguably the most frequently used graphic rating scale is shown in Table 6.1, which attempts to flesh out the five performance levels. This generic form asks the rater to consider how well the individual being rated has met expectations about the job responsibilities. A principal concern is that the form assumes that both the employee and the rater(s) have understood and share a clear set of expectations about performance standards. While most performance appraisal systems are based on this assumption, in our experience all too often this is not the case.

Figure 6.2 An Anchored Graphic Rating Scale

RATING OF TEAMWORK

Works effectively with others in activities where collaboration is essential for task completion..

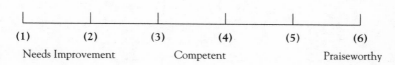

| (1) | (2) | (3) | (4) | (5) | (6) |
| Needs Improvement | | | Competent | | Praiseworthy |

Table 6.1 A Graphic Rating Scale Focused on Meeting Expectations

Rating	Level	Verbal Anchors
1	Expectations not met	• Does not meet expectations in at least four major job responsibilities. • Has received at least one disciplinary action. • Retention of this employee detrimental to organization morale. • Must show clear signs of improvement to avoid termination.
2	Minimal expectation met; needs improvement	• Does not meet expectations in at least two major job responsibilities. • Has received at least one formal, documented verbal or written warning. • Subject to formal disciplinary action if no obvious improvement demonstrated.
3	Expectations met	• Meets expectations in all job responsibilities. • Any prior performance concerns resolved. • Maintenance of present level of performance is expected. • Overall adequate performance.
4	Exceeds expectations	• Exceeds expectations on most job requirements. • Is an informal or formal leader in work unit. • Performance level is a model for other employees in work unit. • Likely candidate for promotion.
5	Far exceeds expectations	• Consistently exceeds expectations for all major job responsibilities. • Demonstrates a high degree of initiation in work-unit and organization-wide activities. • Strong candidate for early promotion or career-enhancing role.

Rarely does an employee have a clear picture of what is expected, and even more rarely do employees and those rating that employee's performance share a common understanding. Further, using such a form requires that the rater(s) are familiar with the employee's performance record before conducting the rating.

An important concern of this type of rating is that the observer will specify which of the major job responsibilities should be considered. Thus, different raters may decide to use different job responsibilities in their evaluations. Despite the increased specificity of this type of rating, this approach too leaves a good bit to be desired.

Problems with Performance Ratings

Given the critical importance of job performance data on both the individual and organizational level, it is not surprising that the establishment of job performance levels is a highly political act in most organizations. On the one hand, senior management is always eager to control costs and increase margins by establishing high levels of job performance while, on the other hand, rank-and-file employees are concerned about setting sweat-shop levels. The HR function charged with setting these standards often finds itself caught in the cross-fire of these competing expectations.

Resolving such conflicts requires developing standards of job performance, taking into account that the standards set are both reasonable and sustainable. In the long run, standards that are set too low breed a complacency, placing the organization at a competitive disadvantage. Developing a realistic set of job performance standards requires both a high level of thoughtfulness and a seriousness of purpose, together with clearly articulated and transparent procedures for achieving them.

Among the various other problems involved in developing performance ratings, we will discuss only a couple of the major ones. One such problem occurs when the individual being rated is well known by the rater(s) for a particular behavior, positive or negative. This knowledge has a generalized impact, coloring the ratings for that individual, even on behaviors that are not relevant to that specific behavior. For example, an employee known throughout the organization for being sociable and gregarious may be rated as highly productive, safety-minded, and extremely conscientious despite there being a lack of evidence to support such ratings. This phenomenon is known as the *halo effect* and can be either positive (when the known behavior is seen as positive) or negative (when the reverse is true).

Another persistent problem with rating scales is the *distributional errors* that result from the raters generally being too lenient or too tough in their judgments. These errors occur when raters have inaccurate frames of reference regarding the markers of different levels of performance. While such errors can be reduced by careful training, providing the raters with clear behavioral anchors for various levels of performance is a more reliable method.

A brief example of the other issues includes, first, the *similar-to-me error*, where the rater assumes the person being rated shares the same values and attitudes and thus exhibits the same behavior as the rater. Second, the *first-impression error* occurs when the rater places too much reliance on his or her first impression of the person being rated. And in a classic review of the research literature on performance ratings Landy and Farr (1988) concluded that a variety of other psycho-social factors played a significant role in the quality of the rating process: the personal characteristics of the rater; the gender, race, and age of both the rater and the persons being evaluated, the status of the rater—peer versus supervisor; and the rater's previous experience with the individual being rated. These conclusions have largely been supported in a more recent review by Latham and Mann (2006).

The many problems with rating scales cited above and others have led to search for an approach that transcends these problems, one that provides reliable and valid measures of performance. Behaviorally anchored ratings scales have provided us with such a tool.

Behaviorally Anchored Rating Scales (BARS)

Behaviorally anchored rating scales (BARS) based on critical incident descriptors were initially developed by Flanagan (1954). Similarly, graphic rating scales produce an evaluation process that yields greater employee acceptance as they are based on behaviors exhibited on the specific job being evaluated. That is, job performance is evaluated in terms of specific behaviors critical to success on this job rather than general traits or abstractions. Anchoring the ratings with specific job behaviors also reduces rater bias and errors. While developing BARS is a time-consuming and labor-intensive process, the benefits from using the method clearly justify the necessary investment,

The BARS method was initially developed by Smith and Kendall (1963) who used behavioral descriptors as a way to construct unambiguous anchors for rating scales. Constructing BARS initially requires collecting critical incidents by direct observation as a way of identifying specific behavioral examples of successful performance and failures. Our current understanding, however, is that critical incidents recalled by others are as valid and useful as those directly observed. The following is a partial list of behavioral incidents collected from supervisors in developing BARS for an administrative assistant:

- Made last-minute travel arrangements enabling an executive to attend critical meeting.
- Opened a letter clearly marked "Confidential. Eyes Only!"
- Corrected typographic and grammatical errors in important document.
- Filed documents in wrong folder and was unable to retrieve them promptly.

These are but of a few of the types of critical incidents that are obtainable from supervisors about job performance that provide anecdotal evidence supporting Sashkin's (1981) conclusion that supervisors are arguably the best source of such information, although other subject-matter experts (SMEs) can provide useful data as well.

How to Implement the BARS Method

The obvious first step is to convene an SME panel of eight to ten persons familiar with this specific job, guided by an experienced facilitator who should explain the purpose of the meeting and then initially ask them to develop individually a list of those behaviors that they have seen over the years that have clearly led to either success or failure on this job. Each of these items should be posted by the facilitator on a flip chart and, when all the individual items have been posted, the group should be encouraged to add others that have occurred to them during the posting.

An HR professional should then take these items and review them for clarity, grammar, and consistency of style and to eliminate redundancies. Additional behavioral incident descriptors should be written as necessary to fill in the obvious gaps, especially incidents that represent borderline behaviors at both ends of the continuum. It is important that the behavioral incidents reported be objective, neutral, and free from an evaluative language such as "poor," "less than," "superior," and so on that would telegraph a conclusion regarding the organizational impact.

The next step is to have the individual members of a new SME panel sort these incidents into categories that are to be used to establish a set of performance dimensions, each with illustrative examples drawn from the collected critical incidents. These dimensions must be edited and examined for clarity and consistency. Sashkin (1981) suggests that these dimensions must be reviewed with four questions in mind:

1. Does this dimension clearly describe an aspect of job performance?

2. Is this an important aspect of job performance?

3. Are these job dimensions independent of each other with little or no overlap?

4. Have any important dimensions of job performance been omitted?

While the answers to these questions are always subjective, they nevertheless are important and must be answered before proceeding. The list of job performance dimensions needs to be edited and refined until appropriate answers emerge.

The third step involves testing the reliability of the sorting of the behaviors into dimensions. A new, third, SME panel is asked to individually take each of the incidents and sort them into one of the newly established dimensions. A 70 percent agreement on the dimension to which an incident belongs is necessary for the process to proceed. When this level of agreement has not been reached, a discussion among the members of the SME panel usually resolves the matter.

Finally, within each of these new dimensions, the SME panel needs to place each of the behaviors along a nine-point (stanine) continuum from outstanding to inadequate performance. Since the process may focus on behaviors at the ends of a continuum of performance, the SME panel may need to develop incidents that describe the middle ranges of job performance.

An example of behaviorally anchored rating scale for teamwork is presented in Figure 6.3. The behavioral incidents are arranged along a nine-point continuum with a rating of "9" indicating outstanding performance and a rating of "1" indicating deficient performance. And, as is usually the case, there are more critical incidents at the two extremes than at the mid-point and, in this case, there may be fewer incidents provided between the mid-point and the two extremes. If these are regarded as necessary, they would need to be developed by the SME panel.

Figure 6.3 A Behaviorally Anchored Ratings Scale

TEAMWORK

	Regularly helps co-workers who are behind in their work.
	Generally provides assistance to co-workers, even when it involves extra time and effort.
9	Shows new employee where to go for lunch, where to find supplies, and generally establishes and maintains good relationships with co-workers.
	Volunteers for difficult or time-consuming team assignments, such as team leader, steering committee member, or team representative.
8	
7	
6	
5	Introduces new employees to co-workers. Has generally positive relationships with co-workers. Participates in team discussions. Avoids people with whom he or she has had previous conflicts, in order to avoid future disagreements.
4	
3	
2	
	Usually behaves as a sole producer rather than a team member.
	Regularly complains about co-workers.
	Will pair up with a co-worker or person against another and pass on critical rumors to stir up controversy.
1	Often ignores requests for assistance.
	After completing special training, does not share new knowledge with co-workers, even if asked.
	Does not participate in team discussions.

A Recommended Shortcut

When the results of a job analysis are available, the process of establishing job performance levels can be shortened. While the process of collecting the behavioral incidents in Step 1 is unchanged, the steps identified above can be eliminated. Instead, the competencies identified during the job analysis should be used for sorting the behaviors.

The importance ratings should be used to choose which of the competencies to include in the job performance. For most jobs it will only be necessary to use performance level 4 or 5 competencies and their identified behaviors to establish levels of performance.

Thus, the SME panel is provided with a list of the pre-determined important job competencies and asked individually to place each of the items into one of the competencies. The facilitator should then post these individual results and resolve differences by having the panel come to a consensus about in which category the behavior belongs.

Once each of the critical incidents has been assigned to an appropriate competency, then each item can be assigned a numerical rank as described above. The final step is for the HR professional to edit the document for clarity, appropriate language, and elimination of redundancies and then have the resulting product critiqued by potential qualified users. Obviously, a formal document with appropriate instructions then needs to be developed.

Applying the BARS Method

Using the BARS method for performance evaluation typically involves independent raters comparing the known behaviors of the individual being rated with the incidents anchoring the points along the BARS. In other words, where along this nine-point scale would this individual's behaviors lead him or her to be placed?

The BARS approach to setting performance standards can be expected to result in a fairer, more accurate, and more defensible performance management system, but only if that system is well implemented. Thus, we have moved in our discussion from a rating scale with no anchoring points, other than a single word, to one that provides a variety of specific behaviors that illustrate the competencies that should guide an evaluation of that individual's job performance. No single method will resolve the problems inherent in an inadequate, biased system. But there can be little question that BARS ratings are a significant improvement over the types ratings that were described earlier in this chapter.

When installing BARS as a new process for establishing performance levels, it is important to begin by gaining organizational acceptance of this method. HR professionals should identify the existing data sources to be used, as well as whatever new sources need to be developed. All data sources that will be used need to be credible and cost-effective. While the benefits to be derived from installing BARS should be highlighted, the time and costs should not be minimized.

BARS and the Hierarchy of Jobs

It is important to recognize that, as one moves along the job hierarchy from entry level to senior management, the number of dimensions important to successful job performance increases, as do the number and complexity of the critical incidents usually involved in each of the dimensions. In Figures 6.4 through 6.7, we present four sets of performance levels for the Problem Solving competency, together with the relevant behavioral items for each. Problem solving is important for each of these job levels—entry, production operations, first-line supervision, and senior management—but how it is expressed varies. These four samples illustrate these differences, how both number and the complexity of behaviors increases as we move from rather simple to more complex jobs. These examples should also provide some additional useful examples of critical incidents that should help sharpen the reader's understanding of this methodology.

Looking at each of these figures shows that those behavioral items at the top end of the list are more problem focused, more likely to produce solutions to problems, and that such solutions are more likely to produce long-lasting, systemic solutions than those at the bottom. As we move from the entry-level jobs to

Figure 6.4 Entry-Level Performance Levels

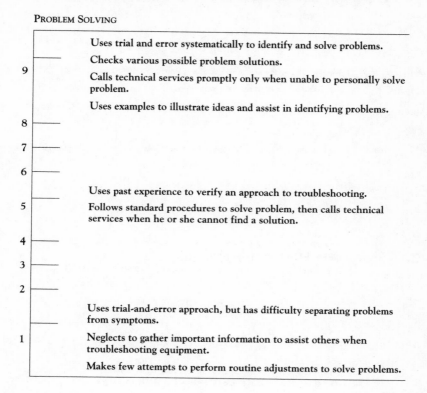

PROBLEM SOLVING

	Uses trial and error systematically to identify and solve problems.
	Checks various possible problem solutions.
9	Calls technical services promptly only when unable to personally solve problem.
	Uses examples to illustrate ideas and assist in identifying problems.
8	
7	
6	
	Uses past experience to verify an approach to troubleshooting.
5	Follows standard procedures to solve problem, then calls technical services when he or she cannot find a solution.
4	
3	
2	
	Uses trial-and-error approach, but has difficulty separating problems from symptoms.
1	Neglects to gather important information to assist others when troubleshooting equipment.
	Makes few attempts to perform routine adjustments to solve problems.

those of senior management, it is also clear that the nature of the behavioral items change from the fairly concrete and specific to the more complex and abstract reflecting the differences in the tasks confronting individuals at these different levels.

Concerns About BARS

Our experience, coupled with many years of research, clearly supports the conclusion that a competently developed set of BARS will provide reliable, readily acceptable levels of job performance and will result in fairer and more accurate understanding of what constitutes job success. But, as we noted earlier, developing such scales is both time-consuming and labor-intensive. And equally

Figure 6.5 Production Operations Performance Levels

PROBLEM SOLVING

9	Observes and listens to a piece of new equipment to get a feel for normal operation.
	Recognizes early warning signs of equipment malfunction.
	Quickly detects maintenance problems.
	Checks equipment operation after a repair activity has been completed.
	Isolates possible causes of a problem and checks each possibility until problem is solved.
	Troubleshoots equipment and puzzles out how a piece of equipment was assembled before attempting repair.
8	
7	
6	
5	Recognizes when equipment malfunction is an indication of materials rather than equipment problems.
	Recognizes a potential machine breakdown only after observing obvious signs of malfunctioning.
4	
3	
2	
1	Overlooks that machine parts are wearing badly and neglects to check the operation of a critical piece of equipment while making rounds.
	Has difficulty in separating problems from symptoms and, as a result, leaves the real problem unsolved.
	Repeatedly makes same adjustments to correct a problem and, after failing to correct the problem, is at a loss as to what else to do.
	Generally tries to solve problems by trial and error and will disassemble a machine in the process of troubleshooting, rather than thinking through the possibilities beforehand.

importantly, despite the quality of the BARS themselves, the fact remains that BARS *are* rating scales. Raters can still ignore the behavioral anchors in making their rating and produce biased and unfair ratings.

But some of these issues can be addressed by training raters to concentrate on the anchors and then to document their ratings

Figure 6.6 Supervisory Performance Levels

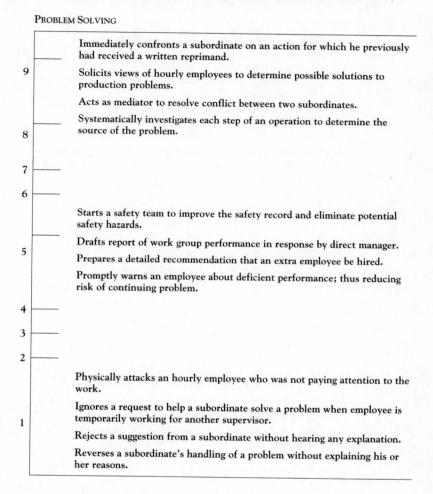

PROBLEM SOLVING

9 — Immediately confronts a subordinate on an action for which he previously had received a written reprimand.

Solicits views of hourly employees to determine possible solutions to production problems.

Acts as mediator to resolve conflict between two subordinates.

8 — Systematically investigates each step of an operation to determine the source of the problem.

7 —

6 —

5 — Starts a safety team to improve the safety record and eliminate potential safety hazards.

Drafts report of work group performance in response by direct manager.

Prepares a detailed recommendation that an extra employee be hired.

Promptly warns an employee about deficient performance; thus reducing risk of continuing problem.

4 —

3 —

2 —

1 — Physically attacks an hourly employee who was not paying attention to the work.

Ignores a request to help a subordinate solve a problem when employee is temporarily working for another supervisor.

Rejects a suggestion from a subordinate without hearing any explanation.

Reverses a subordinate's handling of a problem without explaining his or her reasons.

by including brief, narrative examples of behaviors exhibited by the person being rated that justify that rating. Such a requirement means that raters must have an in-depth knowledge of the person being rated, take their task seriously, and be granted sufficient time to conduct the necessary observations and prepare their ratings. Both the raters and the organization must take this responsibility seriously and, once that is understood throughout the organization, the reputation of the performance management

Figure 6.7 Senior Management Performance Levels

PROBLEM SOLVING

	Constantly monitors events and activities to identify problem situations as they arise.
	Aware of potential consequences of unresolved problems.
	Analyzes the magnitude of situations and appropriately decide who should become involved.
9	Identifies problems in related areas and notifies key individuals to alert them to problems.
	Distinguishes between symptoms and causes.
	Identifies and secures relevant information from different sources to solve problems.
8	
7	
6	
	Identifies problems or situations but responds in an ad hoc fashion.
	Defers action until problems reach a critical threshold before taking action.
5	Attends to crisis situations but overlooks problems that could be solved earlier with less effort.
4	
3	
2	
	Overlooks problem situations.
	Focuses on symptoms rather than on identifying causal factors.
1	Fails to obtain important pieces of information that would lead to a permanent solution.

system will be greatly enhanced. The successful use of BARS depends on the quality of its implementation; the same can be said of most efforts at organizational innovation or change.

A SUMMARY OF THE JOB ANALYSIS PROCESS

A thorough, competent job analysis is the keystone of the entire human resource management process. Without understanding the nature of each specific job in an organization, it is not possible to recruit, select, evaluate, train, develop, and promote or terminate an employee competently. In the preceding pages we have described a process that, if followed, will produce a job analysis that provides this critically important information.

The process that we have described includes four necessary elements: (1) recognize the work activities involved in a job; (2) identify the necessary competencies—the knowledge, skills, and abilities—necessary to perform those work activities; and (3) determine the characteristics of the workplace that are likely to impact job performance; and (4) establish several, objectively determined levels of job performance. The necessary steps to carry out each of these processes are spelled out and a set of materials is provided in the Appendices to this book to facilitate the work of the HR professional in doing so.

We strongly believe that following these steps will produce job analyses that will stand up to review, both by employees within the organization and by those responsible for ensuring that an organization engages in fair, objective human capital management practices.

References

American Educational Research Association, American Psychological Association, National Council on Measurement in Education. (1999). *Standards for educational and psychological testing*. Washington, DC: Author.

Barrick, M.R., & Mount, M.K. (1991). The big five personality dimensions and job performance: A meta-analysis. *Personnel Psychology, 44*, 1–26.

Barrick, M.R., Mount, M.K., & Judge, T.A. (2001). Personality and performance at the beginning of the new millennium: What do we know and where do we go next? *International Journal of Selection and Assessment, 9*, 9–30.

Burke, W.W. (1993). *Organization development: A process of learning and changing* (2nd ed.). Reading, MA: Addison-Wesley.

Burke, W.W. (2002). *Organization change: Theory and practice*. Thousand Oaks, CA: Sage.

Campion, M.A., Palmer, D.K., & Campion, J. (1997). A review of structure in the selection interview. *Personnel Psychology, 50*, 655–702.

Campion, M.A., Pursell, E.D., & Brown, B.K. (1988). Structured interviewing: Raising the psychometric properties of the employment interview. *Personnel Psychology, 41*, 25–42.

Cascio, W.F. (1987). *Applied psychology in personnel management*. Englewood Cliffs, NJ: Prentice Hall.

Costa, P.T., Jr., & McCrae, R.R. (1992). Four ways five factors are basic. *Personality and Individual Differences, 13*, 653–665.

Deal, T.E., & Kennedy, A.A. (2000). *Corporate cultures*. New York: Perseus Books.

Delbecq, A.L., Van de Ven, A.H., & Gustafson, D.H. (1975). *Group techniques for program planning: A guide to nominal group and Delphi processes*. Glenview, IL: Scott, Foresman.

Digman, J.M. (1990). Personality structure: Emergence of the five-factor model. In M.R. Rosenzweig & L.W. Porter (Eds.), *Annual Review of Psychology, 41*, 417–440.

Fine, S.A. (1989). *Functional job analysis scale: A desk aid.* Milwaukee, WI: Author.

Fine, S.A., & Cronshaw, S.F. (1999). *Functional job analysis: A foundation for human resources management.* Mahwah, NJ: Lawrence Erlbaum Associates.

Flanagan, J.C. (1954). The critical incident technique. *Psychological Bulletin, 51,* 327–358.

Fleishman, E.A. (1996). *The Fleishman-job analysis survey (F-JAS).* Potomac, MD: Management Research Institute.

Goodstein, L.D., & Lanyon, R.I. (2007). *JobCLUES: Technical and administrative manual* (Version 3.1). Woodstock, GA: Psichometrics International, LLC.

Goodstein, L.D., & Lanyon, R.I. (1999). Applications of personality assessment to the workplace. *Journal of Business and Psychology, 13,* 291–322.

Goodstein, L.D., & Prien, E.P. (2006). *Using individual assessments in the workplace: A practical guide for HR professionals, trainers, and managers.* San Francisco, CA: Pfeiffer.

Gottfredson, L.S. (1991). The evaluation of alternative measures of job performance. In A.K. Wigdor & B.F. Green, Jr. (Eds.), *Performance assessment for the workplace. Volume II: Technical issues.* Washington, DC: National Academy Press.

Harvey, R.J. (1991). Job analysis. In M.D. Dunnette & L.M. Hough (Eds.), *Handbook of industrial and organizational psychology* (2nd ed.) (Vol. 2, pp. 71–163).

Hofstede, G., & Hofstede, G.J. (2005). *Cultures and organizations: Software of the mind* (2nd ed.) New York: McGraw-Hill.

Hughes, G.L., & Prien, E.P. (1989). Evaluation of task and job skill linkage judgments used to develop test specifications. *Personnel Psychology, 42,* 283–292.

Landy, F.J., & Farr, J.L. (1988). Performance ratings. *Psychological Bulletin, 87,* 72–107.

Latham, G.P., & Mann, S. (2006). Advances in the science of performance appraisal: Implications for practice. In G.P. Hodgkinson & J.K. Ford (Eds.), *International review of industrial and organizational psychology 2006* (Vol. 21). Hoboken, NJ: John Wiley & Sons.

McCormick, E.J., & Jeanneret, P.R. (1988). Position analysis questionnaire (PAQ). In Gael S (Ed.), *The job analysis handbook for business, industry, and government* (Vol. II, pp. 825–842). Hoboken, NJ: John Wiley & Sons.

McCormick, E.J., Mecham, R.C., & Jeanneret, P.R. (1977). *Technical manual for the position analysis questionnaire (PAQ) (System II).* Logan, UT: PAQ Services.

Morgan, G. (2006). *Images of organizations.* (updated ed.) Thousand Oaks, CA: Sage.

Pearlman, K. (1980). Job families: A review and discussion of their implications for personnel selection. *Psychological Bulletin, 87,* 1–28.

Ployhart, R.E., Schneider, B., & Schmitt, N. (2006). *Staffing organizations: Contemporary practice and theory.* Mahwah, NJ: Lawrence Erlbaum Associates.

Prien, E.P. (1977). The function of job analysis in content validation. *Personnel Psychology, 30,* 167–174.

Prien, E.P. (1989). Measuring work setting characteristics: Basis for organizational development. *Human Resources Planning, 12,* 331–337.

Prien, E.P., Prien, K.O., & Gamble, L.G. (2004). Perspectives on nonconventional job analysis methodologies. *Journal of Business and Psychology, 18,* 337–348.

Reiter-Palmer, R., Young, M., Strange, J., Manning, J., & James. J. (2006). Occupationally specific skills: Using skills to define and understand jobs and their requirements. *Human Resources Management Review, 16,* 356–375.

Sashkin, M. (1981). *Assessing performance appraisal.* San Francisco, CA: Pfeiffer.

Schein, E.H. (2004). *Organizational culture and leadership* (3rd ed.) San Francisco, CA: Jossey-Bass.

Smith, P.C., & Kendall, L.M. (1963). Retranslation of expectations: An approach to the construction of unambiguous anchors for rating scales. *Journal of Applied Psychology, 47,* 149–155.

Society for Industrial and Organizational Psychology, Inc. (2004). *Principles for the validation and use of personnel selection procedures* (4th ed.). Bowling Green, OH: Author.

Uniform guidelines on employee selection procedures. (1978). *Federal Register, 43,* 38390–38315.

Wilson, M.A. (2007). A history of job analysis. In L.L. Koppes (Ed.), *Historical perspectives in industrial and organizational psychology.* Mahwah, NJ: Lawrence Erlbaum Associates.

Appendix A

SAMPLE JOB DESCRIPTION

Position Description

Executive Secretary

Summary. The Executive Secretary works under the general supervision of the Executive Vice President. The individual in this position enters data and processes written material; files and retrieves materials; performs administrative secretarial duties; performs reception activities; receives, ships, and distributes mail and supplies; analyzes, interprets, and reports business data; performs other duties as assigned.

Duties

1. Types and processes written material: enters data from copy, long-hand notes, or dictation; composes routine correspondence or memoranda following standard operating procedures; composes letters, memos, or other documents for the executive vice president's signature; prepares tables, charts, graphs, or diagrams based on data provided by other sources.

2. Files and retrieves materials: reviews, updates, or analyzes current status of subject; places forms, records, correspondence in the file; classifies or sorts correspondence, records, or other items following standard office procedure; searches indices, manuals, files, or records for desired information on specific subjects; locates and retrieves files.

3. Performs administrative duties: notifies or reminds the executive vice president or other department heads of meetings, scheduled dates, specific duties, or occurrences; maintains appointment schedule for the executive vice president; coordinates the scheduling of meetings, facilities, or events with other individuals; investigates the source of discrepancies in documentation; prepares travel authorization and or meeting arrangements for departmental personnel.

4. Performs reception activities: answers telephone and screens calls for the executive vice president; greets visitors to the executive vice president's office; answers questions or provides information directly or by telephone.

5. Receives, ships, and distributes mail and supplies: certifies, registers, insures or completes forms associated with special mail services such as overnight courier or registered mail; prepares confidential documents for shipment via courier, distributes mail bulletins, memos, and reports to other employees.

6. Analyzes, interprets, and reports business data: prepares reports, based on information at hand, following standard departmental procedures; prepares analysis or summaries of programs, reports, specific operational items, or other data.

7. Performs other duties as assigned.

Competency Requirements

1. *Communication Skills*: Ability to organize and convey information orally and in documents.

2. *Work and Organization Skills*: Ability to follow through on assignments, adjust schedules, and set priorities.

3. *Scheduling and Coordinating Skills*: Skill in making arrangements, scheduling, coordinating, and orchestrating activities.

4. *Processing Written Materials*: Skill in data entry and proofing copy; knowledge of proper formats for various documents.

5. *Clerical Research and Evaluation Skills*: Knowledge of procedures to locate and obtain materials and to trace sources of errors.

6. *Work and Organization Adaptation*: Ability to pace work activities and to identify, accommodate, and adapt to the conditions or circumstances of the work and the organization and other people.

Minimum Qualifications. Completion of a two-year course of study in secretarial sciences at an accredited institution. A minimum of three years of full-time experience regularly involving at least four of the duty areas in the job description.

Appendix B

ENTRY-LEVEL JOB ANALYSIS TEMPLATES

Target Job Title:_____

1. Name of Analyst:_____

2. Location:_____

3. Analyst's Job Title:_____

4. Time in present position (years):_____ (months):_____

5. Time with company (years):_____ (months):_____

This procedure is designed to identify those job activities and competencies most important for entry-level jobs. The information from this template will be used to conduct a job-related selection assessment for this position.

There are two templates. Template B.1 contains a list of activities that may or may not be an important part of the target job. You will be asked to rate each statement as to that activity's importance for the job. On the next page there is a rating scale and a brief explanation of how to use it.

Template B.2 contains a list of competencies statements. The focus of that part is to determine which competencies are necessary for doing this job successfully. Specific instructions for rating these requirement statements appear following the instructions for rating the job activities.

The key points you should keep in mind as you go through this template are

1. Your judgment and your ratings are to be based on the job as it is now actually performed, not as it might ideally be done.

2. Your judgment should be your own independent judgment. Do not ask anyone else how you should rate an item. Whether it is judged to be important or not is your decision, not anyone else's.

3. If you simply cannot make an honest, accurate rating, leave the item blank.

Importance Ratings: Work Activities

In this section, you are to rate the importance of different work activities with respect to this job. For each statement, proceed in two steps.

1. Consider whether a work activity is or is not part of the job. If it is not part of the job, rate the task "0."

2. If the activity is one that is done by an individual in the job, decide how important it is in that job. Consider the activity in terms of its importance for fully effective job performance.

Use the following scale to make your judgments:

0   This rating indicates that the work activity is never done and is not part of the job.

1   This rating indicates that the work activity has only minor importance relative to other activities performed by individuals in this job. Considering all activities, it would have the lowest priority or importance.

2   This rating indicates that the work activity has a relatively low level of importance compared to other job activities.

3   This rating indicates that the work activity is moderately important for fully effective job performance relative to other activities, and has about average priority among all activities performed.

4   This rating indicates that the work activity is very important to fully effective job performance. It has a higher degree of importance or priority than most other activities.

5   This rating indicates that the work activity is one of the few most essential activities performed. It is one of the most critical aspects of the job.

Template B.1 Entry-Level Importance Ratings: Work Activities

Plan and Organize

1 _____ Work with team members to organize assigned tasks.

2 _____ Determine the general nature of a job through discussion with others doing the same work.

3 _____ Break down work assignment into sequential steps to ensure accuracy and completeness.

Solve Problems

4 _____ Work with team members to troubleshoot and solve problems.

5 _____ Seek assistance when standard procedures are not successful in solving problems.

Manage Personal/Interpersonal Relations

6 _____ Work cooperatively with others.

7 _____ Observe other workers on a team to learn and practice work tasks and skills.

8 _____ Respond to requests for assistance from co-workers or customers/clients.

9 _____ Empathize with others experiencing personal difficulty.

10 _____ Observe and anticipate needs of others without waiting for them to request assistance.

Understand Verbal Communications

11 _____ Meet with supervisor(s) to receive and discuss work assignments.

12 _____ Greet customers/clients and respond to them accurately and appropriately.

13 _____ Remain attentive when receiving instructions, and follow directions or seek clarification when necessary.

14 _____ Respond to crew leader instructions to carry out assignments.

15 _____ Discuss work assignments with co-workers to assess progress or status.

Construction Helper

16 _____ Provide general assistance to experienced craftsperson such as getting requested tools, holding materials in place for additional work, etc.

17 _____ Disassemble and remove worn or damaged materials or structures.

18 _____ Prepare new parts or materials for installation or construction.

19 _____ Complete basic construction or installation.

20 _____ Use basic tools and equipment.

Template B.1 (Continued)

21 _____ Order and/or pick up needed materials, equipment, etc.

22 _____ Clean up shop or work area, machines, equipment, etc.

Manufacturing Production and Maintenance

23 _____ Straighten/clean up working area by removing debris or unused materials.

24 _____ Jog machinery electrically or by hand to put in proper position for alignment/adjustment or to determine the cause of mechanical locks.

25 _____ Adjust panel controls to produce changes in machine timing, smoothness of operations, sequences, or other operating characteristics.

26 _____ Operate machine controls, such as knobs, dials, or levers, to adjust machine operating characteristics.

27 _____ Place or load material into a machine feed system and actuate machine to perform operations until material is consumed.

28 _____ Remove or off-load finished product from machine and place in stacks, containers, or material handling equipment.

29 _____ Obtain raw material or supplies from storage area, staging area, or materials handling equipment and return to work area.

Nursing Aides, Orderlies, Attendants

30 _____ Turn or reposition bedridden patients to prevent bedsores.

31 _____ Feed patients unable to feed themselves and assist them in moving in and out of bed, walking, exercising, etc.

32 _____ Monitor patients' conditions, such as vital signs and food/liquid input/output, and document and report to professional staff.

33 _____ Answer patient call signals.

34 _____ Collect specimens such as urine, feces, sputum and supply and empty bedpans.

35 _____ Clean rooms and change linens.

36 _____ Prepare, serve, and collect food trays.

37 _____ Transport patients from room for specialized services or treatments and return.

Dishwasher

38 _____ Wash dishes, glassware, flatware, and/or pans using dishwashers or by hand.

(continues)

Template B.1 (Continued)

39 _____ Store clean dishes, etc.

40 _____ Maintain kitchen work areas and equipment in clean and orderly condition.

41 _____ Sweep and scrub floors.

42 _____ Sort and remove trash to designated containers/areas and keep garbage cans clean.

43 _____ Transfer supplies and equipment between storage and work areas.

44 _____ Set up banquet tables.

Clerical Assistant

45 _____ Handle outgoing mail tasks: sort outgoing mail as required; prepare necessary forms for registered, insured, overnight, etc., mail and dispatch; arrange and dispatch courier mail.

46 _____ Sort and distribute incoming and internal mail.

47 _____ Greet visitors and answer telephone: provide information and/or direct callers and visitors appropriately.

48 _____ Monitor security camera screens to inspect approaching visitors or detect and report suspicious activity.

49 _____ Sort and file records, forms, correspondence, etc., following established system.

50 _____ Locate, retrieve information from files and send to requestor, searching for missing information as necessary.

51 _____ Maintain records of incoming/outgoing material according to established system and procedures.

52 _____ Complete various standard forms such as checks, receipts, invoices, time or cash reports, etc. and process appropriately.

53 _____ Code information from various sources and prepare for data entry.

54 _____ Enter coded data into database, accounting program, or other.

55 _____ Verify data entered into computer file and correct errors according to standard procedure.

56 _____ Operate and/or maintain various types of office equipment such as printers, copy machines, packaging and mailing equipment, etc.

57 _____ Prepare and process standard mailings to multiple addressees.

58 _____ Prepare standard packages of materials including several items for various purposes such as attendees at a meeting or conference, information for a select list of recipients, etc.

Importance Ratings: Competencies

On the following pages you are to rate the importance of each job requirement. Importance should be judged in terms of how necessary this knowledge, skill, or ability is in order to do the job at a fully effective level of performance. For each requirement statement, proceed in two steps.

1. Consider whether or not the identified competency, that is, knowledge, skill, or ability, is necessary for effective performance of this job. If it is not required at all, you should rate the item a "0."

2. If the identified competency *is* required, then decide how important that competency is to fully effective job performance.

   Use the following scale to make your judgments:

0   This rating indicates that this competency is not necessary for job performance.

1   This rating indicates that this competency has only minor or incidental importance for effective job performance. It is not essential to doing the job, but may occasionally be useful for doing some minor part of the job.

2   This rating indicates that this competency is desirable and useful for doing some minor part of the job but is not important to successfully meeting the major demands of the job.

3   This rating indicates that this competence is moderately important to successful job performance.

4   This rating indicates that this competence is very important to successful job performance.

   This rating indicates that this competence is critically important for successful job performance.

Template B.2 Entry-Level Importance Ratings: Competencies

Plan and Organize

1 _____ Ability to report to work regularly and on time.

2 _____ Ability to establish priorities for completing own work assignments.

3 _____ Ability to determine the sequence or priority of steps necessary to accomplish a task.

4 _____ Ability to estimate time and materials necessary to complete a specific task.

5 _____ Ability to adjust activity schedules or assignments in response to changes in conditions or priorities.

6 _____ Ability to organize work activities and coordinate the performance of others on specific activities.

7 _____ Ability to plan and conduct multiple activities within a specified time frame to ensure goal and deadline achievement.

Understand Verbal and Written Materials or Communications

8 _____ Ability to listen actively to others giving full attention, understanding the speaker's concerns, responding appropriately.

9 _____ Ability to read simple instructions or information such as work orders, shop tickets, CRT screen instructions, work assignments, or descriptive material on containers.

10 _____ Ability to understand verbal instructions, work procedures, or other information and to remember and use them.

11 _____ Ability to provide routine verbal or written status or progress reports to supervisor or others in person, by telephone, or email.

12 _____ Sufficient fluency in English or other specified language(s) to communicate with co-workers, customers/clients, or others.

Handle Numerical Data

13 _____ Ability to transcribe numerical information from one document to another.

14 _____ Ability to add, subtract, multiply, and divide.

15 _____ Skill in entering data into computer.

16 _____ Ability to learn procedures and codes used to enter, change, or delete computer data.

Template B.2 (Continued)

Measure and Make Estimates

17 _____ Ability to estimate the weight, dimensions, and/or quantity of objects or materials.

18 _____ Ability to estimate the speed of moving objects or parts.

19 _____ Ability to estimate the size of large objects or areas relative to each other needed for parking a vehicle, handling a stretcher or gurney, moving a box or crate to another location, etc.

20 _____ Ability to judge the distance between oneself and objects, or between objects.

Make Choices and Solve Problems

21 _____ Ability to set priorities for accomplishing tasks.

22 _____ Ability to choose between appropriate and inappropriate ways of doing a task.

23 _____ Ability to make choices or decisions in which the risks and consequences are slight such as sorting materials, storing equipment, etc.

24 _____ Ability to make choices or decisions that affect the security or well-being of others and/or involve serious risk or consequences.

25 _____ Knowledge of standard procedures for solving common problems.

26 _____ Ability to determine that a making a choice or finding a solution should be referred to a supervisor or other person with greater skills or experience.

Follow Safety Procedures

27 _____ Knowledge of basic safety principles for working on or near machinery.

28 _____ Ability to understand and apply information in safety data sheets.

29 _____ Knowledge of measures necessary to protect oneself from job hazards and ability to use them.

30 _____ Understanding of importance of wearing protective clothing items and willingness to do so.

31 _____ Skill in working under potentially hazardous conditions such as on slippery surfaces, with wet equipment, etc.

(continues)

Template B.2 (Continued)

Use Tools and Measuring Instruments

32 _____ Ability to use basic hand tools as required such as screwdrivers, dollies, pliers, etc.

33 _____ Ability to perform operations not requiring great accuracy using hammer, wrench, trowel, putty knife, cleaning equipment, etc.

34 _____ Ability to operate powered, hand-held tools or implements to perform operations requiring accuracy, such as pencil grinder, drill, or miniature soldering iron.

35 _____ Ability to measure existing parts or conditions with a micrometer, blood pressure cuff, or other precision instruments and record or use results as appropriate.

Provide Customer Service

36 _____ Ability to determine customer needs and preferences or requirements.

37 _____ Ability to answer customer questions, suggestions, or complaints tactfully.

38 _____ Ability to provide personal attention and service that enhance customer loyalty and maintain brand image.

39 _____ Ability to recognize and capitalize on social and situational cues that affect customer relations.

Provide Personal Service/Assistance/Support

40 _____ Ability to recognize and respond to non-verbal cues or physical actions indicating a need for assistance.

41 _____ Ability to recognize and respond to signs of personal distress of an individual being assisted.

42 _____ Ability to hold, position, or move an individual who is incapacitated or immobile.

43 _____ Knowledge and understanding of the dependency relationship between a service provider or care giver and the recipient.

44 _____ Knowledge of the factors or conditions that interfere with the long-term health status of a non-communicative or comatose person.

Template B.2 (Continued)

Adapt to Work and Organizational Requirements

45 _____ Ability to pace work activities and maintain the level of attention to detail essential to complete work assignments.

46 _____ Ability to identify, accommodate, and adapt to the conditions and circumstances of the work, the organization, rules and regulations, and relationships with other people to maintain a smooth running and efficient organization.

Construction Helper

47 _____ Knowledge of machines and tools, their proper uses and maintenance, and basic repairs.

48 _____ Basic knowledge of construction materials and methods.

49 _____ Basic troubleshooting and repair skills for standard equipment.

50 _____ Ability to use fingers, hands, and other parts of one's body with steadiness, strength, and coordination.

Manufacturing Production and Maintenance

51 _____ Ability to read and interpret gauges, dials, digital displays.

52 _____ Ability to manipulate hand and/or foot controls.

53 _____ Ability to lift, pour, stir, or otherwise handle raw materials.

54 _____ Ability to inspect finished products for defects, blemishes, or flaws.

55 _____ Basic knowledge of machine operations.

56 _____ Ability to read and follow written instructions to debug machine stoppages.

Nursing Aides, Orderlies, Attendants

57 _____ Basic skills in providing medical care such as taking vital signs, changing dressings, assisting patient with personal care, specimen collection, etc.

58 _____ Skill in using basic medical equipment, including ability to identify malfunction and knowledge of what to do in that case.

59 _____ Ability to observe patients' conditions in order to determine their needs for care and assistance.

60 _____ Skill in actively looking for ways to help patients and co-workers.

(continues)

Template B.2 (Continued)

61 _____ Capacity to sense and respond to needs and preferences of patients from different social, cultural, etc., backgrounds.

62 _____ Knowledge of privacy and confidentiality standards and requirements for medical care providers.

Dishwasher

63 _____ Knowledge of correct use and maintenance of commercial washing, draining, and drying equipment and of trash compacters.

64 _____ Knowledge of correct use and maintenance of related tools and equipment such as various thermometers, dish-cleaning brushes, etc.

65 _____ Knowledge of proper storage for foods and ingredients.

66 _____ Ability to watch gauges, dials, etc. to make sure equipment is working properly.

67 _____ Knowledge of equipment maintenance requirements and ability to perform maintenance and basic repairs.

Clerical Assistant

68 _____ Ability to use standard word processing, database, and/or accounting programs.

69 _____ Skill in sorting various types of information or materials into various categories.

70 _____ Skill in operating and maintaining standard office equipment such as computers, copy machines, printers, packaging and mailing equipment, etc.

Appendix C

PRODUCTION OPERATIONS JOB ANALYSIS TEMPLATES

Target Job Title:_____

1. Name of Analyst:_____

2. Location:_____

3. Analyst's Job Title:_____

4. Time in present position (years):_____ (months):_____

5. Time with company (years):_____ (months):_____

This procedure is designed to identify those job activities and competencies most important for a production operations jobs. The information from this template will be used to conduct a job-related selection assessment for this position.

There are two templates. Template C.1 consists of a list of activities that may or may not be an important part of the target job. You will be asked to rate each statement as to that activity's importance for the job. On the next page there is a rating scale and a brief explanation of how to use it.

Template C.2 contains a list of competencies statements. The focus of that part is to determine which competencies are necessary for doing this job successfully. Specific instructions for rating these requirement statements appear following the instructions for rating the job activities.

The key points you should keep in mind as you go through this template are

1. Your judgment and your ratings are to be based on the job as it is now actually performed, not as it might ideally be done.

2. Your judgment should be your own independent judgment. Do not ask anyone else how you should rate an item. Whether it is judged to be important or not is your decision, not anyone else's.

3. If you simply cannot make an honest, accurate rating, leave the item blank.

Importance Ratings: Work Activities

In this section, you are to rate the importance of different work activities with respect to this job. For each statement, proceed in two steps.

1. Consider whether a work activity is or is not part of the job. If it is not part of the job, rate the task "0."

2. If the activity is one that is done by an individual in the job, decide how important it is in that job. Consider the activity in terms of its importance for fully effective job performance.

Use the following scale to make your judgments:

0   This rating indicates that the work activity is never done and is not part of the job.

1   This rating indicates that the work activity has only minor importance relative to other activities performed by individuals in this job. Considering all activities, it would have the lowest priority or importance.

2   This rating indicates that the work activity has a relatively low level of importance compared to other job activities.

3   This rating indicates that the work activity is moderately important for fully effective job performance relative to other activities, and has about average priority among all activities performed.

4   This rating indicates that the work activity is very important to fully effective job performance. It has a higher degree of importance or priority than most other activities.

5   This rating indicates that the work activity is one of the few most essential activities performed. It is one of the most critical aspects of the job.

Template C.1 Production Operations Importance Ratings: Work Activities

Production Operations

1 _____ Operate machine controls such as knobs, dials, or levers by using one or both hands to perform a linear or rotary motion to adjust machine operations.

2 _____ Operate while seated machine control levers requiring the use of one or both feet to adjust machine operation.

3 _____ Use continuous variable control knobs, dials, or levers to control the process, speed of processing, or speed of material flow based on visual observation of the relevant machine operation.

4 _____ Place or load material into a machine feed system and start machine performing operations until material is consumed.

5 _____ Place material in manufacturing process equipment to a stop position where material is aligned and then actuate machine operation.

6 _____ Place and align material in fixed position in manufacturing process machine using fixtures or visual cues, then begin machine operation.

7 _____ Place material in the feed position and start machine operation while providing continuous feed of material to completion of operation.

8 _____ Remove or off-load finish product from machine and place in stacks or container or material handling equipment.

9 _____ Remove scrap from machine or separate from finished product and place in appropriate storage container.

10 _____ Adjust machine speed based on skill level, product quality checks, or work pace.

11 _____ Adjust machine operations to correct problems in product quality.

12 _____ Move raw material or supplies from storage area, staging area, or materials handling equipment to work area.

13 _____ Position materials and supplies for availability to production equipment operators or for in-process storage.

14 _____ Place raw materials or partially finished products or supplies used by production employees using in-process storage or staging areas.

15 _____ Off-load finished product from materials handling devices and place in appropriate containers.

Template C.1 (Continued)

16 _____ Assemble product packaging materials or containers using tape, glue, or stapling equipment.

17 _____ Operate hand-held or automatic stapling, gluing, taping, or heat-sealing equipment used in product packaging.

18 _____ Classify finished products by color, size, texture, or coded labels, then sort and distribute to the respective holding bins.

19 _____ Place and position work-in-process items on material handling device for next operation and sequence.

20 _____ Rework products to remove blemishes or to complete an unfinished operation to salvage defective items.

21 _____ Inspect product for flaws and classify, sort, and distribute to materials handling or holding bins.

22 _____ Operate equipment to regulate flow, mixing, blending, or transfer of product, chemicals, or gasses.

23 _____ Operate machine controls to coordinate activities of several production, processing, or testing units.

24 _____ Clear machine jams, reload materials, reset fixtures, or otherwise prepare machine to function and restart.

25 _____ Place material or finished product into a continuous operation machine feed system.

Handle Product/Fulfill Orders

26 _____ Prepare products for packaging or packing in shipping containers by cleaning, removing processing labels, folding, wrapping in protective film, or otherwise making ready for shipment.

27 _____ Inspect and grade damaged products or packaging based on extent and nature of damage.

28 _____ Pack and record carton contents on packing list and attach to customer order form or insert in shipping carton.

29 _____ Verify shipping address and contents of orders being dispatched by comparing packing or shipping list and order form, and secure shipping label.

30 _____ Verify contents of returned cartons by comparing to shipping lists.

(continues)

Template C.1 (Continued)

31 _____ Record product information (type, size, location) on work order or inventory control form.

32 _____ Match product information to work order or inventory control form.

33 _____ Complete working forms or production documents containing information needed for subsequent operations or records.

34 _____ Record customer quality complaints on returned merchandise.

35 _____ Sort products by type, size, color, or other characteristics.

36 _____ Select labels to be attached to products according to work orders and attach using sewing machine or bar tack machine.

37 _____ Select product packages from inventory to match customer order and place in shipping carton.

38 _____ Produce labels and maintain an inventory of customer/product labels used to identify items.

39 _____ Inspect packaging materials for quality of print and assembly of package.

Plan, Organize, Schedule, and Coordinate

40 _____ Plan or schedule movement of material or products.

41 _____ Plan or direct projects or major portions of projects.

42 _____ Establish priorities for completing own work.

43 _____ Establish procedures for others to follow in making repairs, maintenance, etc.

44 _____ Assist in instruction of other workers on safe and proper work procedures.

45 _____ Maintain or update logs/records of changes made to operating systems (e.g., control adjustments, parts replaced, time spent, etc.).

46 _____ Inventory parts, tools, fittings, and maintenance stock materials.

47 _____ Develop checklist detailing steps for corrective action on production equipment.

48 _____ Maintain a file of building floor plans, utilities and production equipment, blueprints, and manufacturers' manuals and bulletins.

49 _____ Determine the general nature of a job through discussion with others who have done similar work.

Template C.1 (Continued)

50 _____ Determine the sequence of steps necessary to accomplish a job (e.g., machine setup sequence, starting point for construction, etc.).

51 _____ Determine the types and amounts of materials, equipment, instruments, etc., required to do a job.

52 _____ Identify parts based on part numbers, codes, or other markings.

53 _____ Select nuts, bolts, and other standard hardware with respect to thread size, length, fit, hardness, or other characteristics.

54 _____ Select proper hand tools and other equipment to accomplish a job.

55 _____ Check materials against specifications before beginning work.

56 _____ Read blueprints, drawings, layouts, or schematics to understand the nature of the planned job.

57 _____ Sketch rough drawings to gain a better understanding of the job or to explain the job to others.

Operate Machines and Equipment

58 _____ Perform setup and/or positioning operations prior to machining or welding (by self or others).

59 _____ Operate equipment in motion such as cranes, hoists, or conveyor systems.

60 _____ Operate powered mobile equipment typically not intended for highway use, such as scooter, warehouse truck, or forklift.

61 _____ Operate powered vehicles intended for highway use such as automobile, truck, or bus.

62 _____ Manipulate moving devices such as hand trucks, dollies, wheeled racks, or carts to transport materials within a work area.

Inspect and Troubleshoot

63 _____ Inspect parts or assemblies for proper fit, alignment, part orientation, defects, or errors.

64 _____ Inspect equipment or work products to detect malfunctions or need for repair, adjustment, or lubrication.

65 _____ Inspect products to detect small errors or major imperfections for defects in raw materials, finished products, or packaging.

66 _____ Check fit, binding, pinching, or coordination of parts or assemblies with other parts.

(continues)

Template C.1 (Continued)

67 _____ Inspect machine parts or components to detect excessive heat or vibration.

68 _____ Disassemble parts, components, tools, or assemblies, and reassemble according to sketches, schematics, blueprints, or parts prints.

69 _____ Add or remove production machine covers or assemblies, work aids, etc., according to the requirements of the operators.

70 _____ Determine minimum repairs or modifications necessary to maintain machine or equipment operations on a temporary or emergency basis.

71 _____ Question machine operators to determine possible causes of mechanical, electrical, or electronic failures in order to initiate troubleshooting.

Handle Paperwork

72 _____ Classify or sort informational material, correspondence, records, business forms, merchandise, or other items following standard methods.

73 _____ Maintain or update logs/records of changes made to operating systems, including control adjustments, parts replaced, time spent, and operating status.

74 _____ Search indices, manuals, files, records, or other sources for desired or missing information on specific subjects.

75 _____ Inventory production raw materials parts, tools, fittings, and maintenance stock materials.

76 _____ Look up and interpret numerical or alphabetical codes.

77 _____ Complete forms by filling in information such as part numbers, time spent, department identification, equipment and functioning status.

78 _____ Fill out records of meter or gauge readings.

79 _____ Prepare requisitions for parts, materials, tool room orders, or consumable supplies.

80 _____ Fill out schedules of regular and preventive maintenance performed.

81 _____ Prepare tags to indicate that equipment is out of service.

82 _____ Write notes or make records describing actions taken or providing other information for the benefit of the next person on the job.

Template C.1 (Continued)

83 _____ Log actions taken to repair equipment, complete maintenance, or make adjustments.

84 _____ Record on inventory records the use of machine parts requisitioned from parts inventory.

Perform Maintenance

85 _____ Clean and lubricate equipment/equipment components (zerts and plugs) according to servicing needs or equipment requirements.

86 _____ Remove debris or unused materials to straighten/clean up working area.

87 _____ Inspect and/or change or clean air filters, vents, air lines, regulators, etc., in HVAC systems.

88 _____ Clean screens/filters by flushing and/or draining piping of slime, sludge, or other debris.

89 _____ Install breather tubes, gauges, zert fittings, oil lines, filters, sight glasses, etc.

90 _____ Disassemble, clean, and/or repair steam, water, or oil traps and reassemble.

91 _____ Inspect, clean, and/or replace indicator lamps, display lamps, reflectors, and bulbs.

92 _____ Check and tighten drive chains, keyways, sets screws, bolts, etc.

93 _____ Jog machinery to put in proper position for alignment, adjustment, or to determine the cause of mechanical locks.

94 _____ Adjust panel controls to produce changes in machine timing, smoothness of operations, sequences, or other operating characteristics.

Importance Ratings: Competencies

On the following pages you are to rate the importance of each job requirement. Importance should be judged in terms of how necessary this knowledge, skill, or ability is in order to do the job at a fully effective level of performance. For each requirement statement, proceed in two steps.

1. Consider whether or not the identified competency, that is, knowledge, skill, or ability, is necessary for effective performance of this job. If it is not required at all, you should rate the item a "0."

2. If the identified competency *is* required, then decide how important that competency is to fully effective job performance.

Use the following scale to make your judgments:

0   This rating indicates that this competency is not necessary for job performance.

1   This rating indicates that this competency has only minor or incidental importance for effective job performance. It is not essential to doing the job, but may occasionally be useful for doing some minor part of the job.

2   This rating indicates that this competency is desirable and useful for doing some minor part of the job but is not important to successfully meeting the major demands of the job.

3   This rating indicates that this competence is moderately important to successful job performance.

4   This rating indicates that this competence is very important to successful job performance.

This rating indicates that this competence is critically important for successful job performance.

Template C.2 Production Operations Importance Ratings: Competencies

Handle Written Communications

1 _____ Ability to read simple instructions or information such as work orders, shop tickets, work assignments, computer screen instructions, descriptive material on containers, etc.

2 _____ Ability to read detailed instructions or information such as maintenance manuals, equipment information, or trade textbooks in order to troubleshoot, service, repair production equipment.

3 _____ Ability to read complex material such as engineering handbooks, specifications and standards, or technical literature.

4 _____ Ability to prepare written reports on such matters as equipment malfunction, performance results, or accidents.

5 _____ Ability to prepare detailed memoranda or reports on topics such as historical production data or research findings.

6 _____ Ability to translate technical information into non-technical language for use by management.

7 _____ Ability to present data, interpretation, and conclusions in written form.

8 _____ Ability to write technical specifications and procedures.

Perform Calculations

9 _____ Ability to transcribe numerical information from one document to another.

10 _____ Ability to detect and correct arithmetic errors.

11 _____ Ability to detect errors or discrepancies in the entry of records, posting data, or other log entries.

12 _____ Knowledge of the English and metric standard measurement units and conversion procedures.

Handle Verbal Communication

13 _____ Ability to understand verbal instructions or work procedure information provided by supervisor or others.

14 _____ Ability to receive on-the-job training provided by supervisor or others.

15 _____ Ability to participate in group meetings or training sessions where effectiveness depends on understanding others.

(continues)

Template C.2 (Continued)

16 _____ Ability to identify the important points of information from material presented orally.

17 _____ Ability to communicate with co-workers through conversation or discussion where effectiveness depends on making oneself understood.

18 _____ Ability to provide routine verbal status or progress reports to supervisor or others in person or by telephone.

19 _____ Ability to obtain information through personal interviews or personal conversations with others.

20 _____ Ability to persuade an operator that a machine is not functioning satisfactorily when all indicators are positive.

Understand Graphic Information

21 _____ Ability to read and interpret blueprints or drawings such as detailed assembly or parts drawings.

22 _____ Ability to read solid state schematics or logic diagrams to determine input/output signal requirements, voltage references, etc. for troubleshooting activities.

23 _____ Ability to read pneumatic or hydraulic schematics to identify troubleshooting, repair, or assembly procedures.

24 _____ Ability to read an electrical schematic to identify a sequence of electrical troubleshooting activities.

25 _____ Ability to read a schematic or diagram to determine the proper sequence of equipment assembly and disassembly or for parts replacement.

26 _____ Ability to determine the relationship between physical symptoms of mechanical failure and corresponding points of reference in an electrical drawing or schematic.

Use Computers

27 _____ Knowledge of the procedures used to access computer system programs, enter files, and edit or delete data or information.

28 _____ Skill in using software for diagnosing and repairing system malfunctions.

29 _____ Knowledge of software and techniques for testing equipment, simulating events, and/or isolating equipment malfunctions.

Template C.2 (Continued)

30 _____ Knowledge of procedures for isolating faults in logic circuitry.

31 _____ Knowledge of operating characteristics and malfunctions of photocells, sensors, relays, electrically controlled thermostatic devices, and/or micro switches.

Perceive Differences and Relationships

32 _____ Ability to understand the relationship of physical objects to one another in order to visualize a number of such objects acting together.

33 _____ Ability to detect differences in shapes, shadings, figures, or widths and lengths.

34 _____ Ability to understand mechanical relationships in practical situations such as understanding leverage, how pulleys work, the direction gear arrangements turn, etc.

35 _____ Ability to understand magnification or amplification of linear, rotary, or oscillating movement in parts or equipment.

36 _____ Ability to detect/recognize differences between actual and standard operations of mechanical equipment (e.g., smoothness of operation, play, and backlash in machine parts, etc.).

37 _____ Ability to use mechanical principles to analyze, evaluate, and troubleshoot high-speed production machines with linear, rotary, reciprocating, or oscillating operations and controls.

Make Estimates

38 _____ Ability to estimate the weight of objects.

39 _____ Ability to estimate the size, length, or quantities of small objects such as screws, nails, fasteners, etc.

40 _____ Ability to estimate the size of large objects or areas relative to each other, as in parking a vehicle or moving a crate between machines.

41 _____ Ability to estimate relative differences in the speed of two or more objects, machines, belts, etc.

42 _____ Ability to estimate the speed of moving objects or parts.

43 _____ Ability to judge the distance between oneself and objects, or between objects.

(continues)

Template C.2 (Continued)

Make Choices and Solve Problems

44 _____ Ability to make choices or decisions in which the risks and consequences are slight, such as sorting material/parts or storing apparatus.

45 _____ Ability to make choices or decisions affecting the security or well being of others and/or which involve serious risks or consequences.

46 _____ Ability to solve problems involving a few relatively concrete principles or methods, such as troubleshooting malfunctions or breakdowns in familiar equipment.

47 _____ Ability to solve problems involving a variety of abstract variables by applying scientific principles or logic to define the problem, assemble data, and/or draw valid conclusions.

48 _____ Ability to specify a sequence of activities to locate or retrieve lost or misplaced files, documents, etc.

49 _____ Ability to recognize what specific additional information about a problem or situation should be collected.

Plan, Organize, Schedule, Coordinate

50 _____ Ability to assign priority or sequence to the steps for completing a job.

51 _____ Ability to coordinate the activities of other individuals or departments on joint projects.

52 _____ Ability to schedule multiple projects which compete for limited resources (time, equipment, personnel, etc.).

53 _____ Ability to organize project activities and orchestrate the performance of helpers on specific activities.

Supervise

54 _____ Ability to explain and demonstrate work procedures to others.

55 _____ Ability to evaluate equipment operation in terms of operator time requirements, attention and skill requirements.

56 _____ Ability to recognize waste and loss in use of manpower, material, equipment, machines, etc. to identify or locate areas for potential improvements or savings.

Template C.2 (Continued)

57 _____ Ability to instruct others in the correct methods and procedures for performing maintenance or service tasks by demonstrating, coaching and providing feedback on their performance.

Handle Hand and Power Tools and Measuring Instruments

58 _____ Ability to use screwdriver, Allen wrench or file for making adjustments.

59 _____ Ability to use hammers, wrenches, trowel, putty knifes, and perform operations not requiring great accuracy.

60 _____ Ability to operate powered, hand-held tools or implements to perform operations requiring accuracy, such as pencil grinder, drill, or miniature soldering iron.

61 _____ Ability to operate chain hoists, portable cranes, come-alongs, or other stationary and portable devices to remove, manipulate, or replace heavy equipment and equipment parts.

62 _____ Ability to measure existing parts with a micrometer, Vernier caliper, or other precision instruments to obtain specifications for parts duplication, blueprint preparation, etc.

63 _____ Ability to select and use electric, air, or hydraulic power-driven hand tools, such as drills, grinders, chippers, impact wrenches, sanders, air and electric saws, etc.

64 _____ Ability to use clamps, riggings, stands, etc. to lay out, hold, position, or assemble machine, burn, or weld materials.

Troubleshoot and Repair Mechanical Systems

65 _____ Knowledge of normal operating characteristics of mechanical equipment, such as smoothness of operation, play, and backlash in machine parts, vibration, noise, and heat.

66 _____ Knowledge of the effects of friction on the operation, efficiency and wear of machinery, and procedures to reduce wear and parts failure.

67 _____ Knowledge of the relationships among machine parts and the effects of adjustments made to related machine parts, such as an adjustment to compensate for wear in one part of the machine.

68 _____ Knowledge of the basic principles and laws of motion with reference to linear, circular, rotary, relative, and harmonic motion.

(continues)

Template C.2 (Continued)

69 _____ Knowledge of types and uses of attachments or pieces of equipment used in individually operated production, materials handling, or packaging operations.

70 _____ Knowledge of production machine capabilities (i.e., punch press, drill press, sewing and knitting, woodworking or finishing. equipment) in relation to productivity and quality improvement.

Follow Safety Procedures

71 _____ Knowledge of basic safety principles for working on or near machinery.

72 _____ Knowledge of equipment lockout and other safety procedures.

73 _____ Knowledge of requirements for shields, guards, and protective devices for stationary and portable equipment or machinery.

74 _____ Knowledge of work space design and requirements in relation to worker safety requirements and operations efficiency.

75 _____ Ability to understand and apply information in safety manuals and other sources.

Adapt to Work and Organization Requirements

76 _____ Ability to pace work activities and maintain a sense of urgency and level of attention to detail essential to complete work assignments and achieve goals.

77 _____ Knowledge of proprietary restrictions on discussing organizational operations, plans, problems or relationships with other organizations.

78 _____ Ability to adapt to the conditions and circumstances of work, to adapt to the organization's rules and regulations in order to maintain a smoothly running and efficient organization.

79 _____ Ability to recognize and capitalize on social cues that affect the outcome of business and personal dealings with other people.

Appendix D

CLERICAL JOB ANALYSIS TEMPLATES

1. Name of Analyst:_____
2. Location:_____
3. Analyst's Job Title:_____
4. Time in present position (years):_____ (months):_____
5. Time with company (years):_____ (months):_____

This procedure is designed to identify those job activities and competencies most important for clerical jobs. The information from this template will be used to conduct a job-related assessments for this position.

There are two templates. Template D.1 consists of a list of activities which may or may not be an important part of the target job. You will be asked to rate each statement as to that activity's importance for the job. On the next page there is a rating scale and a brief explanation of how to use it.

Template D.2 contains a list of competency statements. The focus of that part is to determine which competencies are necessary for doing this job successfully. Specific instructions for rating these competency statements appear following the instructions for rating the job activities.

The key points you should keep in mind as you go through this template are

1. Your judgment and your ratings are to be based on the job as it is now actually performed, not as it might ideally be done.

2. Your judgment should be your own independent judgment. Do not ask anyone else how you should rate an item. Whether it is judged to be important or not is your decision, not anyone else's.

3. If you simply cannot make an honest, accurate rating, leave the item blank.

Importance Ratings: Work Activities

In this section, you are to rate the importance of different work activities with respect to this job. For each statement, proceed in two steps.

1. Consider whether a work activity is or is not part of the job. If it is not part of the job, rate the task "0."

2. If the activity is one that is done by an individual in the job, decide how important it is in that job. Consider the activity in terms of its importance for fully effective job performance.

Use the following scale to make your judgments:

0   This rating indicates that the work activity is never done and is not part of the job.

1   This rating indicates that the work activity has only minor importance relative to other activities performed by individuals in this job. Considering all activities, it would have the lowest priority or importance.

2   This rating indicates that the work activity has a relatively low level of importance compared to other job activities.

3   This rating indicates that the work activity is moderately important for fully effective job performance relative to other activities, and has about average priority among all activities performed.

4   This rating indicates that the work activity is very important to fully effective job performance. It has a higher degree of importance or priority than most other activities.

5   This rating indicates that the work activity is one of the few most essential activities performed. It is one of the most critical aspects of the job.

Template D.1 Clerical Job Analysis Importance Ratings: Work Activities

Process Written Materials

1 _____ Send standard letters, printed literature, or other materials in response to routine requests within predetermined limits.

2 _____ Prepare tables, graphs, charts, etc., based on data from other sources.

3 _____ Proofread completed forms or correspondence for inaccuracies in spelling, punctuation, grammar, format, neatness, or general appearance.

4 _____ Produce copies of correspondence, reports, etc., and prepare them for distribution.

5 _____ Forward completed correspondence or business files to supervisor for final review and approval.

6 _____ Prepare material for distribution using machine or by hand, copy, gather, fold, staple, or seal packets/envelopes.

File and Retrieve Materials

7 _____ Review, update, or revise file contents to reflect current status of subject.

8 _____ Place forms, records, correspondence, or other material in the correct location in a systematic file.

9 _____ Classify or sort informational material, correspondence, records, business forms, merchandise, or other items following standard system.

10 _____ Search indices, manuals, files, records, or other sources for desired or missing information on specific subjects.

11 _____ Locate and retrieve filed or stored material.

12 _____ Maintain records of incoming and outgoing materials through use of system and procedures.

13 _____ Retrieve records and/or information from file and forward to others.

Analyze, Interpret, Report

14 _____ Prepare reports based on information at hand following standard procedures.

15 _____ Maintain custody of evidence presented at meetings (including written memoranda, documents, etc.) for incorporation into transcripts and records.

Template D.1 (Continued)

16 _____ Prepare displays (tables, graphs, charts, or diagrams) summarizing numerical or statistical data (e.g., financial data or operating statistics).

17 _____ Locate and retrieve data, records, or other information needed to conduct or complete projects, conducting a search or investigation if necessary.

Transcribe Material

18 _____ Take notes of information to be included in reports, letters, or documents.

19 _____ Transcribe information from recording machine tapes or other material.

20 _____ Take notes in meetings, conferences, or from phone calls to produce minutes, notes, or summary reports.

Solve Problems

21 _____ Work with team members to troubleshoot and solve problems.

22 _____ Seek assistance when standard procedures are not successful in solving problems.

23 _____ Use trial-and-error approach to solving problems when appropriate.

Keep Books

24 _____ Review accounting statements, expense reports, and standard forms for, accuracy, completeness, and conformity to procedures.

25 _____ Allocate debits, credits, costs, charges, or other similar bookkeeping items to correct accounts or classification.

26 _____ Post entries in financial journals, ledgers, or other financial records.

27 _____ Make necessary entries or adjustments to reconcile out of balance account.

28 _____ Verify and process invoices for payment.

29 _____ Assist in internal and external audits of fiscal and financial operations.

30 _____ Assist individuals with account problems by reviewing account information.

31 _____ Produce a trial balance of accounts and locate and correct errors.

(continues)

Template D.1 (Continued)

Code, Transcribe, Enter Data

32 _____ Prepare summary or data entry/coding sheets for computer processing from information contained in other sources.

33 _____ Allocate charges or payments to individual departments and accounts using accounting codes.

34 _____ Verify accuracy of data coding and make necessary corrections.

35 _____ Code materials using number or letter codes.

36 _____ Complete various routine forms such as checks, receipts, invoices, form letter addresses, time or cash reports, etc., according to standard operating procedure.

37 _____ Operate computer peripheral equipment (e.g., printer, scanner, etc.).

38 _____ Verify the accuracy of data entered into computer file using printout or visual screen.

39 _____ Analyze computer or computer equipment operation in relation to conditions displayed on screens, monitors, etc.

Receive and Distribute Mail

40 _____ Certify, register, insure, or complete forms associated with special mail services such as overnight, courier, or registered mail.

41 _____ Arrange for the delivery of confidential documents via courier or special messenger.

42 _____ Sort and deliver mail, materials, or supplies to appropriate individuals.

43 _____ Distribute mail, bulletins, memos, and reports to employees and offices.

Perform Reception Functions

44 _____ Greet visitors and direct them to the appropriate individual.

45 _____ Answer questions and give requested directions or other information directly or by telephone.

46 _____ Verify or confirm the identity of phone callers prior to initiating actions.

47 _____ Receive orders, requests, instructions, or information, personally or by telephone.

48 _____ Sign or initial documents to acknowledge receipt of valuables.

Template D.1 (Continued)

49 _____ Schedule use of facilities and/or equipment and assist individuals in their use.

50 _____ Answer telephone, relay messages, and provide routine information.

51 _____ Monitor remote security camera screens to inspect approaching visitors to detect atypical or suspicious vehicle, activity, or events that occur in a monitored region.

Communicate

52 _____ Select, assemble, and arrange distribution of news articles or other materials (brochures, leaflets, etc.) of interest within the organization.

53 _____ Assist in planning, coordinating, and administering sponsored activities for employees or visitors (e.g., meetings, banquets).

54 _____ Maintain bulletin board or other displays of employee-relevant information.

55 _____ Keep a log of all events occurring during shift and make entries to journal to inform next shift personnel.

56 _____ Create and distribute a regular company newsletter for all staff.

Plan, Organize, Schedule

57 _____ Estimate materials, labor, and time requirements for specific projects.

58 _____ Maintain up-to-date manuals of department/job practices and procedures to standardize the activities of subordinates.

59 _____ Develop sequenced action plans to correct problems with equipment or work processes or procedures.

60 _____ Coordinate multiple and/or competing activities and assignments for efficient use of time and resources.

61 _____ Maintain and keep up-to-date database for financial data, inventory, personnel records, etc.

62 _____ Prepare a roster of individuals' daily shift assignments by unit for use in tracking individuals by activity.

63 _____ Review information from outgoing shift to determine priority items for attention.

(continues)

Template D.1 (Continued)

Operate and Maintain Equipment

64 _____ Conduct scheduled inspections to determine need for equipment maintenance.

65 _____ Arrange maintenance work for office equipment according to an established schedule or priority system.

66 _____ Repair, adjust, clean, and otherwise service electrical and mechanical office machines.

67 _____ Operate the various types of office equipment used by organization.

68 _____ Prepare and distribute or assign work orders for maintenance and repair of facilities, utilities, equipment, or grounds.

Perform Administrative Functions

69 _____ Notify or remind certain individuals or departments of meetings, scheduled dates, specific duties, or occurrences.

70 _____ Maintain an appointment book or schedule for one's supervisor.

71 _____ Coordinate the scheduling of meetings, facilities (conference rooms, etc.), or events (tours, banquets, classes, etc.) with other individuals or groups.

72 _____ Investigate the source of discrepancies in documentation or search for lost documents through coordination with others outside the department.

73 _____ Prepare expense vouchers and travel authorization and complete travel or meeting arrangements for departmental personnel.

Importance Ratings: Competencies

On the following pages you are to rate the importance of each job requirement. Importance should be judged in terms of how necessary this knowledge, skill, or ability is in order to do the job at a fully effective level of performance. For each requirement statement, proceed in two steps.

1. Consider whether or not the identified competency, that is, knowledge, skill, or ability, is necessary for effective performance of this job. If it is not required at all, you should rate the item a "0."

2. If the identified competency *is* required, then decide how important that competency is to fully effective job performance.

   Use the following scale to make your judgments:

0   This rating indicates that this competency is not necessary for job performance.

1   This rating indicates that this competency has only minor or incidental importance for effective job performance. It is not essential to doing the job, but may occasionally be useful for doing some minor part of the job.

2   This rating indicates that this competency is desirable and useful for doing some minor part of the job but is not important to successfully meeting the major demands of the job.

3   This rating indicates that this competence is moderately important to successful job performance.

4   This rating indicates that this competence is very important to successful job performance.

   This rating indicates that this competence is critically important for successful job performance.

Template D.2 Clerical Job Analysis Importance Ratings: Competencies

Communicate

1 _____ Ability to explain and demonstrate work procedures to others.

2 _____ Ability to use information coming from two or more sources simultaneously, such as listening to a customer's concern and paying attention to an intercom.

3 _____ Sufficient fluency in English or other specified language to communicate with co-workers and customers or clients.

4 _____ Ability to coordinate work with co-workers through conversation/discussion where effectiveness depends on understanding others.

5 _____ Ability to understand spoken instructions or work procedures provided by supervisor or others.

6 _____ Ability to participate in group meetings or training sessions where effectiveness depends on understanding others.

7 _____ Ability to provide routine verbal status or progress reports to supervisor or others in person.

8 _____ Ability to make informal reports or presentations to small groups.

9 _____ Ability to obtain information through personal interviews or personal conversations.

10 _____ Knowledge of what information should be considered confidential.

11 _____ Ability to convey information in a concise fashion without loss of necessary detail.

12 _____ Ability to organize information in reports, correspondence, etc., in a logical and meaningful manner.

13 _____ Ability to maintain or project a positive image in face-to-face conversations as well as in telephone conversations.

14 _____ Ability to calmly, politely, and firmly handle unsolicited communications from disturbed individuals.

15 _____ Ability to respond to multiple, simultaneous communications requiring quick reaction.

Handle Quantitative Data

16 _____ Ability to accurately recognize and recall a series of numbers (e.g., telephone numbers, zip codes, account codes).

17 _____ Ability to compare objects, letters, symbols, and numbers to determine identity or degree of similarity.

Template D.2 (Continued)

18 _____ Skill in following procedures to count money and make change for cash transactions.

19 _____ Ability to transcribe numerical information from one document to another.

20 _____ Ability to detect and correct arithmetic errors.

21 _____ Ability to detect errors or discrepancies in the entry of records, posting data, or other log entries.

22 _____ Skill in use of a calculator to perform basic arithmetic calculations (adding, subtracting, multiplying, dividing).

23 _____ Skill in using a calculator to perform multi-step arithmetic calculations, including use of memory functions.

24 _____ Ability to perform calculations involving algebraic or statistical formulas or other complex procedures used in handling business data.

Handle Written Material

25 _____ Ability to read and use simple instructions or information such as work orders, work assignments, computer screen instructions, or descriptive material on containers.

26 _____ Ability to read and use detailed instructions or information such as maintenance manuals, equipment information, or trade textbooks in order to troubleshoot, service, and repair equipment.

27 _____ Ability to read and understand complex material such as technical handbooks, specifications and standards, or technical literature.

28 _____ Ability to read and comprehend professional journals and legal publications and to apply concepts, policies, and procedures to work activities.

29 _____ Ability to read and use computer commands, codes, and instructions.

30 _____ Ability to follow established sequence of written procedures for start-up and operation of various types of equipment.

31 _____ Ability to enter simple information on forms or to otherwise record data according to standardized instructions such as recording dates, codes, quantities, or number of errors.

32 _____ Ability to prepare simple records such as work reports, inventory data, or information for next shift.

33 _____ Ability to prepare written records such as equipment malfunction, performance results, or accident data.

(continues)

Template D.2 (Continued)

34 _____ Ability to prepare detailed memoranda or reports such as summary reports or project results.

35 _____ Ability to combine information from multiple sources into a final report.

36 _____ Knowledge of rules of grammar and punctuation.

37 _____ Ability to detect errors in grammar, punctuation, or omissions through proofing letters, reports, forms, tables, or codes.

38 _____ Ability to spell commonly used English words and business and legal terms.

Manage Personal/Interpersonal Relations

39 _____ Relate courteously to customers/clients and co-workers.

40 _____ Skill in expressing apologies or explanations for the inconveniences of others.

41 _____ Ability to negotiate priorities with individuals in the organization.

42 _____ Ability to predict the reaction of others to information, events, or conditions.

43 _____ Skill in the application of timing, tact, and discretion in communicating business-related information.

44 _____ Ability to recognize and capitalize on social and interpersonal cues in dealing with others.

45 _____ Ability to focus attention on work assignments or responsibilities in a distracting environment.

46 _____ Knowledge of factors that affect timely completion of work assignments.

Work Within Organization

47 _____ Ability to adjust schedules to reflect changing situations, requirements, or priorities.

48 _____ Ability to work without close supervision.

49 _____ Ability to recognize the impact of what other employees are doing upon one's own area of responsibility.

50 _____ Ability to interpret and implement instructions issued from management.

51 _____ Ability to follow through on specific problems or programs and maintain a continuous level of emphasis until completion.

52 _____ Ability to work effectively with others in close or stressful situations.

Template D.2 (Continued)

53 _____ Ability to maintain complex clerical records and prepare reports from such records.

54 _____ Knowledge of standard office procedures and basic filing methods and materials.

Enter Data

55 _____ Ability to enter, change, or delete computerized information.

56 _____ Skill in operating computer peripherals such as printers, scanners, etc.

57 _____ Ability to use specified computer software programs.

58 _____ Skill in typing from manuscript, draft copies, voice recordings, or dictation.

59 _____ Skill in recording the proceedings or minutes of meetings or conferences with multiple speakers.

Keep Books

60 _____ Knowledge of procedures used to credit or debit accounts and post general ledger entries.

61 _____ Ability to detect errors or discrepancies in the entry of records, posting data, or other log entries.

62 _____ Knowledge of procedures used to calculate principle, interest, taxes, fees, discount and payment schedules.

63 _____ Knowledge of standard bookkeeping and accounting principles and procedures.

64 _____ Knowledge of procedures for handling time cards and preparing payroll records and documentation.

65 _____ Skill in accurately making cash transactions accurately, including making change for cash payments.

66 _____ Ability to process large sums of money and make a variety of cost computations.

Plan, Organize, Schedule

67 _____ Ability to breakdown a complex situation into its primary components.

68 _____ Skill in making the arrangements, scheduling, and completing other details for meetings.

69 _____ Ability to plan and conduct multiple activities within a specified time frame to ensure achieving goals and meeting deadlines.

(continues)

Template D.2 (Continued)

70 _____ Ability to evaluate and choose between conflicting alternatives based on partial or incomplete information.

71 _____ Ability to adjust project schedules or work assignments in response to changes in conditions or priorities.

Make Choices and Solve Problems

72 _____ Ability to set priorities for accomplishing tasks.

73 _____ Ability to choose between appropriate and inappropriate ways of doing a task.

74 _____ Ability to make choices or decisions in which the risks and consequences are slight such as sorting materials, storing equipment, etc.

75 _____ Knowledge of standard procedures for solving common problems.

76 _____ Ability to determine that a making a choice or finding a solution should be referred to a supervisor or other person with greater skills or experience.

Adapt to Work and Organization

77 _____ Knowledge of the protocol regarding meetings, conferences, events, appointments, and authority relationships.

78 _____ Knowledge of the restrictions and proprietary standards regarding discussion of organization operations, plans, problems, or relationships with other organizations.

79 _____ Knowledge of organizational standards regarding dress, language, personal hygiene, attendance, and expressed attitudes toward co-workers, customers/clients, or others.

80 _____ Ability to distinguish between problems that can be resolved through routine procedures from those that require specialized response or attention of other persons.

81 _____ Ability to identify, accommodate, and adapt to the conditions and circumstances of the work, the organization, rules and regulations, and relationships with other people to maintain a smooth-running and efficient organization.

82 _____ Ability to maintain attention and pace of work activities when performing repetitive tasks or when confronted by distractions, competing requirements, or persons.

Appendix E

SALES AND SALES MANAGEMENT JOB ANALYSIS TEMPLATES

1. Name of Analyst:_____
2. Location:_____
3. Analyst's Job Title:_____
4. Time in present position (years):_____ (months):_____
5. Time with company (years):_____ (months):_____

This procedure is designed to identify those job activities and competencies most important for sales and sales management jobs. The information from this template will be used to conduct a job-related assessment for this position.

There are two templates. Template E.1 consists of a list of activities that may or may not be an important part of the target job. You will be asked to rate each statement as to that activity's importance for the job. On the next page there is a rating scale and a brief explanation of how to use it.

Template E.2 contains a list of competency statements. The focus of that part is to determine which competencies are necessary for doing this job successfully. Specific instructions for rating these requirement statements appear following the instructions for rating the job activities.

The key points you should keep in mind as you go through this template are

1. Your judgment and your ratings are to be based on the job as it is now actually performed, not as it might ideally be done.

2. Your judgment should be your own independent judgment. Do not ask anyone else how you should rate an item. Whether it is judged to be important or not is your decision, not anyone else's.

3. If you simply cannot make an honest, accurate rating, leave the item blank.

Importance Ratings: Work Activities

In this section, you are to rate the importance of different work activities with respect to this job. For each statement, proceed in two steps.

1. Consider whether a work activity is or is not part of the job. If it is not part of the job, rate the task "0."

2. If the activity is one that is done by an individual in the job, decide how important it is in that job. Consider the activity in terms of its importance for fully effective job performance.

Use the following scale to make your judgments:

0   This rating indicates that the work activity is never done and is not part of the job.

1   This rating indicates that the work activity has only minor importance relative to other activities performed by individuals in this job. Considering all activities, it would have the lowest priority or importance.

2   This rating indicates that the work activity has a relatively low level of importance compared to other job activities.

3   This rating indicates that the work activity is moderately important for fully effective job performance relative to other activities, and has about average priority among all activities performed.

4   This rating indicates that the work activity is very important to fully effective job performance. It has a higher degree of importance or priority than most other activities.

5   This rating indicates that the work activity is one of the few most essential activities performed. It is one of the most critical aspects of the job.

Template E.1 Sales and Sales Management Importance Ratings: Work Activities

Prospect

1 _____ Evaluate prospect potential, service requirements, and other factors to develop sales plans and goals.

2 _____ Advise customers of the advantages of adding additional products based on sales and marketing information.

3 _____ Estimate sales based on trends in sales or restocking product at various customers.

4 _____ Assist customers in setting up new stores by conducting and coordinating promotional activities.

5 _____ Determine adjustments, refunds, and discounts, then balance to reconcile sales records.

6 _____ Evaluate and select advertising from options provided by agency and placement in media.

7 _____ Establish boundaries of sales territories based on geographical area, customer base, accessibility, volume, sales strategy, or other factors.

8 _____ Set-up and staff trade show booths or exhibits to present product information and make contact with prospective buyers or clients.

9 _____ Set-up and maintain a schedule that provides adequate coverage of both existing customer base and new customer development.

10 _____ Prepare prospecting strategies or action plans based on relevant information.

11 _____ Work with customers' employees on ways to promote and upsell products.

12 _____ Analyze customer inventory and sales data and recommend changes and adjustments to purchasing patterns.

13 _____ Explain benefits of products and services to prospective or actual customers.

Monitor and Analyze

14 _____ Develop action plans for customers to achieve and maintain proper inventory levels of our products.

15 _____ Recommend modifications in company sales and marketing to meet changing situations, such as the need for new products or responding to competitors' activities.

Template E.1 (Continued)

16 _____ Monitor sales territory performance and make needed adjustments to maintain sales and market share.

17 _____ Attend trade shows to gain information on industry activity, products, and trends.

18 _____ Regularly evaluate customer needs in order to establish priorities for sales calls, service, product delivery, etc.

19 _____ Analyze sales data on competitors' products to provide management with information needed for decision making.

20 _____ Discuss POS display possibilities and promotional options with customers.

21 _____ Analyze sales data using various approaches, such as by product or by customer, to identify potential problems.

22 _____ Inspect display shelves to remove damaged product and correct misplaced product according to agreed-upon specifications.

23 _____ Investigate delays in payment for service or product to ensure customer compliance with purchase agreements.

24 _____ Assess competitor activity through personal contact with individuals and observation outside the company.

25 _____ Analyze customer business conditions, climate, and competition with reference to company programs.

26 _____ Prepare and evaluate sales proposals for programs, including products, facilities, services, benefits, and costs.

27 _____ Identify potential business opportunities and threats to current or future sales for incorporation in the overall strategy.

Implement

28 _____ Develop business opportunity ideas into detailed action programs to maintain or improve sales.

29 _____ Prepare and deliver sales presentations describing products and services, promotions, and advertising.

30 _____ Assess retailer sales performance through interviews with consumers and retail store personnel.

31 _____ Set up and maintain special sales and seasonal displays.

(continues)

Template E.1 (Continued)

32 _____ Maintain records of demand for products, sales aids, or other materials needed for meeting sales goals.

33 _____ Develop advertising and promotional materials in accordance with marketing strategy and sales goals.

34 _____ Contact individuals in customer organizations to answer questions or obtain information related to sales proposals, delivery, pricing, etc.

35 _____ Identify customer objections to new product or service proposals.

36 _____ Identify slow moving products to understand reasons and develop action plans, such improving or eliminating product, etc.

37 _____ Evaluate physical layout of retail outlets for proper placement of POS.

38 _____ Prepare status reports on sales, distribution, pricing, inventories, special programs, etc., for review by management.

39 _____ Analyze customer requirements and market conditions to develop sales proposals.

Overcome Objections

40 _____ Establish business and personal contacts with decision makers and others in the customer organization and keep them informed of new or impending developments in product, pricing, etc.

41 _____ Explain company strategy, its marketing and merchandising positions to customers to stimulate customer business development.

42 _____ Monitor reports of industry activities from various sources to identify threats or opportunities that can impact the company.

43 _____ Identify individuals within a customer organization who have responsibility and authority for purchasing or contracting decisions.

44 _____ Forecast sales and market penetration based on historical data, sales strategy, and competitor activity in the sales territory.

45 _____ Assist customers in their sales activities by keeping them informed of new products or price specials.

46 _____ Analyze and interpret retailer performance reports and/or forecasts to identify trouble spots for future management action.

47 _____ Negotiate and close sales.

Template E.1 (Continued)

Plan, Organize, Schedule, Coordinate

48 _____ Maintain daily schedule including entries for inventory, sales by product, and customer information.

49 _____ Make oral presentations to senior management analyzing and reviewing market conditions, factors affecting sales, and sales activity.

50 _____ Initiate sales contracts, purchase agreements, and other financial arrangements.

51 _____ Monitor expenditures to identify trends and evaluate variances in relation to sales goals and budgets.

52 _____ Adjust work schedules or project priorities to meet emergencies or changing conditions.

53 _____ Develop personal long-range goals and plans for sales promotion programs, dealing with specific customers, new projects, etc.

54 _____ Prepare reports or memos detailing and explaining deviations from sales goals.

55 _____ Participate in meetings with others from the company to coordinate plans and decisions.

56 _____ Propose or review proposed strategies and objectives to be included in long-range business plans.

Sales Management—Supervise

57 _____ Assign sales representatives to particular territories in order to meet sales goals, fulfill sales strategies, and accommodate personal preferences.

58 _____ Identify personal interests and abilities that provide a competitive advantage for a sales representative.

59 _____ Motivate sales personnel to increase sales.

60 _____ Modify territories (on the basis of size, demographics, performance, etc.) in order to implement strategies and reach sales goals.

61 _____ Organize and/or conduct sales meetings/training of sales representatives to develop product knowledge, increase morale, recognize outstanding performance, etc.

(continues)

Template E.1 (Continued)

64 _____ Evaluate subordinates' performance against established guidelines, objectives, and performance standards and provide action-oriented feedback to correct deficiencies.

63 _____ Interview candidates for sales positions to determine their qualifications and suitability for employment.

64 _____ Establish sales territories based on workload, priorities, and capabilities of individual sales personnel.

65 _____ Develop and implement procedures for evaluating the performance of sales department to identify needed changes.

66 _____ Conduct exit interviews to determine causes for separation and to identify trends that have policy implications.

67 _____ Set performance objectives for sales force and monitor progress toward those objectives.

Sales Management—Coordinate, Organize, Communicate

68 _____ Coordinate trade show/convention activities to ensure proper coverage and product exposure.

69 _____ Seek out assistance or guidance from superiors or peers when faced with unusual or unfamiliar situations without clear solutions.

70 _____ Develop and maintain up-to-date manuals of sales department policies and procedures.

71 _____ Investigate recurrent disputes among sales personnel to determine causes and resolve such disputes.

72 _____ Keep sales force up-to-date on sales and merchandising programs.

73 _____ Organize and coordinate team selling efforts.

74 _____ Coordinate multiple and/or competing activities and assignments for efficient use of time and resources.

75 _____ Conduct training programs for employees to develop their technical skills or to introduce new procedures.

76 _____ Obtain and clarify information from employees relevant to work procedures and standards.

77 _____ Assess and evaluate the adequacy of manpower resources, internal business controls, equipment, and facilities.

Template E.1 (Continued)

78 _____ Review personnel data to discern trends in absenteeism, tardiness, or turnover to facilitate development of personnel policies.

79 _____ Prepare or interpret personnel policies, procedures, rules, and regulations to employees.

80 _____ Maintain a calendar of events relating to sales, promotional, or marketing activities.

Sales Management—Plan Strategy

81 _____ Develop marketing strategies including features that emphasize benefits, price points, product mix, etc.

82 _____ Develop action plans to implement sales and marketing strategies.

83 _____ Monitor company sales programs and operations to identify training needs and develop programs to meet these needs.

84 _____ Conduct staff meetings to exchange information, define objectives, establish priorities, and develop solutions for emerging problems.

85 _____ Analyze business operation or project requirements to determine individual roles and make work assignments.

86 _____ Develop action plans containing costs, critical dates, and required activities for completion.

87 _____ Develop budget projections and recommendations based on business plans and strategies.

88 _____ Develop and implement modifications in sales procedures or approaches to correct or contain budget variances.

89 _____ Monitor and evaluate workload of subordinates to determine optimum allocation, priorities, and schedule for an organizational unit.

90 _____ Prepare or review contracts, purchase agreements, and other financial arrangements.

91 _____ Review and evaluate customer relations programs to determine their effectiveness.

Importance Ratings: Competencies

On the following pages you are to rate the importance of each job requirement. Importance should be judged in terms of how necessary this knowledge, skill, or ability is in order to do the job at a fully effective level of performance. For each requirement statement, proceed in two steps.

1. Consider whether or not the identified competency, that is, knowledge, skill, or ability, is necessary for effective performance of this job. If it is not required at all, you should rate the item a "0."

2. If the identified competency *is* required, then decide how important that competency is to fully effective job performance.

Use the following scale to make your judgments:

0   This rating indicates that this competency is not necessary for job performance.

1   This rating indicates that this competency has only minor or incidental importance for effective job performance. It is not essential to doing the job, but may occasionally be useful for doing some minor part of the job.

2   This rating indicates that this competency is desirable and useful for doing some minor part of the job but is not important to successfully meeting the major demands of the job.

3   This rating indicates that this competence is moderately important to successful job performance.

4   This rating indicates that this competence is very important to successful job performance.

This rating indicates that this competence is critically important for successful job performance.

Template E.2 Sales and Sales Management Importance Ratings: Competencies

Prospect

1 _____ Skill in developing information to identify and qualify sales prospects.

2 _____ Skill in developing information about new prospects.

3 _____ Skill in analyzing existing accounts to determine potential for additional sales.

4 _____ Skill in balancing and/or reconciling sales totals, inventory figures, etc.

5 _____ Ability to secure cold call appointments by telephone.

6 _____ Ability to analyze competitive product lines to determine appropriate competitive selling strategies.

7 _____ Ability to analyze the features and benefits of a competitor's product line to determine areas of vulnerability.

8 _____ Ability to stimulate interest in a product or service in a face-to-face cold call.

Monitor and Analyze

9 _____ Skill in gathering information about a competitor's activity, products, or services.

10 _____ Ability to analyze a customer's sales and profit structure to obtain information for preparing sales calls.

11 _____ Skill in asking questions to identity issues or concerns that prevent closing a sale.

12 _____ Skill in asking questions to qualify a customer to identify needs.

13 _____ Ability to recognize subtle cues that suggest a customer's opinion or judgment regarding a product or service that is for sale.

Make Presentations

14 _____ Ability to actively involve and interest prospective customers when making sales presentations.

15 _____ Ability to involve a group of potential customers when making a sales presentation.

16 _____ Ability to recognize when a change in focus or direction of a sales presentation is necessary.

17 _____ Ability to stage or create events in sales presentations that capitalize on the commitment of one or more individuals to the recommended product or service.

(continues)

Template E.2 (Continued)

18 _____ Ability to evaluate and respond to the comments and/or cues of other sales representatives in team selling efforts.

19 _____ Ability to determine the degree of formality or propriety appropriate to a sales call.

20 _____ Ability in a sales call to stress the importance of personal attention and service in the future.

21 _____ Ability to project a positive image in telephone conversations with customers.

22 _____ Ability to control the sequence and timing of events in a sales call.

23 _____ Ability to project an appearance of self-confidence in dealing with prospective or actual customer.

24 _____ Skill in organizing information and materials needed for sales calls.

Integrate Information

25 _____ Ability to evaluate the value and compatibility of products and/or services offered for a customer's business operations.

26 _____ Ability to evaluate the impact of competitive activity on future sales of product/services.

27 _____ Ability to identify individuals within a client organization who have the authority to make purchasing decisions.

28 _____ Ability to identify potential sales objections by evaluating customer qualifying information.

29 _____ Skill in analyzing a customer's needs and preferences to determine the proper timing and frequency of sales calls.

30 _____ Ability to identify the business and personal factors that influence a customer's purchasing decisions.

31 _____ Ability to determine the impact of changes in a client organization on current or future sales.

32 _____ Ability to analyze the profit structure of competitive product lines to determine appropriate competitive selling strategies.

33 _____ Ability to recognize the comments or other cues provided by a customer that indicate a competitor's efforts at displacement selling.

34 _____ Ability to evaluate sales potential, qualifying information, and level of resistance to sales efforts.

35 _____ Ability to evaluate customer vulnerability to competitive selling.

Template E.2 (Continued)

Overcome Objections and Close

36 _____ Ability to recognize the need to obtain further information in order to satisfy a customer's sales objections.

37 _____ Ability to respond directly and succinctly to a sales objection.

38 _____ Skill in describing a point of view that is contrary to the views or opinions of a customer.

39 _____ Ability to recognize the appropriate timing for summarizing and/or closing a sales presentation.

40 _____ Ability to recognize the appropriate level of forcefulness needed to obtain a product or service purchasing commitment.

41 _____ Skill in adjusting the sequence and timing of a sales presentation in response to a customer's objections.

42 _____ Skill in handling points of contention in a sales presentation.

43 _____ Skill in identifying possible tradeoffs in negotiations with customers.

44 _____ Skill in negotiating adjustments and terms of sales contracts and closing sales.

Plan, Organize, Schedule, Coordinate

45 _____ Ability to shift selling or administrative priorities in response to changed schedules or conditions.

46 _____ Ability to schedule and manage day-to-day personal job activities.

47 _____ Skill in organizing and maintaining various sales files and records.

48 _____ Ability to share or divide attention between different projects or activities.

49 _____ Ability to prioritize sales activities when faced with conflicting alternatives.

50 _____ Ability to attend to the details of record keeping requirements (e.g., customer activity, product use, sales calls made, etc.).

51 _____ Ability to prioritize sales development activities in response to customer qualifying information.

Follow-Up

52 _____ Ability to convey an understanding of its importance in responding to customer complaints or problems.

53 _____ Skill in describing the features and benefits of intangibles, including technical services, promotional advertising, etc.

(continues)

Template E.2 (Continued)

54 _____ Ability to address or respond to customer's problems without compromising the company's position or creating liability.

55 _____ Ability to determine the benefit of continued sales activity with a customer based on customer qualifying information, other selling opportunities, etc.

56 _____ Skill in obtaining payments to resolve delinquent accounts or other customer credit problems.

57 _____ Skill in addressing past service problems in a way that maintains customer confidence in company products or services.

58 _____ Ability to respond to customer complaints and maintain composure in stressful circumstances.

Merchandise

59 _____ Skill in designing visual aids for management and/or sales presentations.

60 _____ Ability to design sales aids that demonstrate an understanding of a customer's business operation, resources, and concerns.

61 _____ Skill in setting up and maintaining retail point of sale displays and merchandise.

62 _____ Ability to evaluate brand representation and movement in retail store outlets.

63 _____ Ability to recognize the usefulness of different sales materials, promotional devices, etc., for prospecting and sales activities.

64 _____ Skill in evaluating the physical layout of retail outlets for proper placement of point of sale displays and merchandise.

65 _____ Ability to estimate product or package sales for special events or seasonal activities.

Handle Customer Relations/Sales Support

66 _____ Skill in giving formal technical instructions to customers' employees.

67 _____ Ability to write technical specifications and procedures to be included in sales proposals.

68 _____ Ability to describe the features and benefits of a technically complex product or service in a way that is appropriate to the technical knowledge and competence of the customer.

69 _____ Ability to evaluate technical data to solve a customer's systems problems.

70 _____ Ability to identify and resolve causes of technical problems in a customer's operations.

Template E.2 (Continued)

Sales Management—Supervise

71 _____ Ability to successfully interview and choose competent sales personnel.

72 _____ Skill in motivating a sales force to increase sales.

73 _____ Ability to assign sales personnel to appropriate sales territories.

74 _____ Skill and willingness to evaluate subordinates' performance against sales goals.

75 _____ Skills in setting sales goals and monitoring progress in meeting these goals.

76 _____ Skill in organizing and conducting sales meetings to develop product knowledge, increase morale, recognize outstanding performance, and so on.

77 _____ Knowledge of when and how to develop and modify sales territories in response to changing demographics, losses of sales personnel, etc.

78 _____ Ability to determine reasons for personnel losses by conducting and analyzing exit interviews.

Sales Management—Coordinate, Organize, Communicate

79 _____ Ability to select and organize trade show/convention activities to produce product exposure and acceptance.

80 _____ Ability to conceptualize, write, and produce sales manuals and related materials.

81 _____ Skill in coordinating multiple and/or competing sales activities.

82 _____ Ability to organize and coordinate team selling efforts.

83 _____ Ability to work effectively with sales personnel from diverse backgrounds.

84 _____ Ability to assess and evaluate human resources, business controls, sales programs, and other elements to mount and manage an effective sales program.

85 _____ Ability to develop, conduct, and evaluate sales training programs.

86 _____ Skill in working with sales staff to determine sales trends, customer problems, and other important information.

87 _____ Skill in maintaining a calendar of sales and promotional events.

Sales Management—Plan Strategy

88 _____ Ability to develop marketing strategies including features that emphasize benefits, price points, product mix, etc.

(continues)

Template E.2 (Continued)

89 _____ Skill in developing action plans to implement sales and marketing strategies.

90 _____ Ability to monitor company sales programs and operations to identify training needs and develop programs to meet these needs.

91 _____ Skills in conducting staff meetings to exchange information, define objectives, establish priorities, and develop solutions for emerging problems.

92 _____ Ability to develop action plans involving estimates of costs, setting critical dates, and identifying required activities.

93 _____ Skill in developing budget projections and recommendations based on business plans and strategies.

94 _____ Ability to develop and implement modifications in sales procedures or approaches to correct or contain budget variances.

95 _____ Skills in monitoring and evaluating workload of subordinates to determine optimum allocations, priorities, and schedule for sales units.

96 _____ Ability to prepare or review contracts, purchase agreements, and other financial arrangements.

97 _____ Ability to review and evaluate customer relations programs to determine their effectiveness.

Adapt to Work and Organizational Requirements

60 _____ Knowledge of organizational practices and norms regarding meetings, events, appointments, authority relationships, and organizational structure.

61 _____ Knowledge of the relationships, dependencies, and contingencies among organizational units, key management positions, and other positions and functions.

62 _____ Knowledge of the proprietary standards regarding discussion of company operations, plans, problems, and professional relations with other organizations.

63 _____ Knowledge of the norms and practices regarding verbal expression and behavior in professional or social settings where the individual is identified with the organization.

64 _____ Knowledge of the formal and informal standards regarding dress, language, personal hygiene, attendance, and expressed attitudes when identified with the organization.

65 _____ Ability to differentiate settings, conditions, or circumstances that determine when the individual is identified with the organization or is functioning as a private citizen.

Appendix F

CLERICAL/ADMINISTRATIVE SERVICES JOB ANALYSIS TEMPLATES

1. Name of Analyst:_____
2. Location:_____
3. Analyst's Job Title:_____
4. Time in present position (years):_____ (months):_____
5. Time with company (years):_____ (months):_____

This procedure is designed to identify those job activities and competencies most important for clerical and administrative jobs. The information from this template will be used to conduct a job-related selection assessment for this position.

The template consists of two parts. Template F.1 consists of a list of activities which may or may not be an important part of the target job. You will be asked to rate each statement as to that activity's importance for the job. On the next page there is a rating scale and a brief explanation of how to use it.

Template F.2 contains a list of competencies statements. The focus of that template is to determine which competencies are necessary for doing this job successfully. Specific instructions for rating these requirement statements appear following the instructions for rating the job activities.

The key points you should keep in mind as you go through this template are

1. Your judgment and your ratings are to be based on the job as it is now actually performed, not as it might ideally be done.

2. Your judgment should be your own independent judgment. Do not ask anyone else how you should rate an item. Whether it is judged to be important or not is your decision, not anyone else's.

3. If you simply cannot make an honest, accurate rating, leave the item blank.

Importance Ratings: Work Activities

In this section, you are to rate the importance of different work activities with respect to this job. For each statement, proceed in two steps.

1. Consider whether a work activity is or is not part of the job. If it is not part of the job, rate the task "0."

2. If the activity is one that is done by an individual in the job, decide how important it is in that job. Consider the activity in terms of its importance for fully effective job performance.

Use the following scale to make your judgments:

0   This rating indicates that the work activity is never done and is not part of the job.

1   This rating indicates that the work activity has only minor importance relative to other activities performed by individuals in this job. Considering all activities, it would have the lowest priority or importance.

2   This rating indicates that the work activity has a relatively low level of importance compared to other job activities.

3   This rating indicates that the work activity is moderately important for fully effective job performance relative to other activities, and has about average priority among all activities performed.

4   This rating indicates that the work activity is very important to fully effective job performance. It has a higher degree of importance or priority than most other activities.

5   This rating indicates that the work activity is one of the few most essential activities performed. It is one of the most critical aspects of the job.

Template F.1 Clerical/Administrative Services Importance Ratings: Work Activities

Typewritten Materials Importance

1 _____ Proofread reports or other correspondence for grammar or spelling.

2 _____ Send standard letters, printed literature, or other materials in response to routine requests within predetermined limits.

3 _____ Compose letters, memos, or other documents for the supervisor's signature from notes or following general instructions.

4 _____ Type tables, graphs, charts, or diagrams, based on data supplied from other sources.

5 _____ Type drafts and final copy of legal documents, contracts, letters, or records.

6 _____ Type letters, memos, reports, or other documents from manuscript or rough draft, dictation tape, or shorthand notes.

File and Retrieve Materials

7 _____ Review, update, or revise file contents to reflect current status of subject.

8 _____ Place forms, records, correspondence, or other material in the correct location in a systematic file.

9 _____ Classify or sort informational material, correspondence, records, business forms, merchandise, or other items following standard methods of systematized arrangement.

10 _____ Search indices, manuals, files, records, or other sources for desired or missing information on specific subjects.

11 _____ Locate and retrieve filed or stored material.

12 _____ Maintain records of incoming and outgoing materials through use of cataloging system, computerized circulation system, and withdrawal file.

13 _____ Retrieve records and/or information from file and submit to other agencies.

Take Dictation

14 _____ Take shorthand notes of material to be included in reports, letters, or documents.

15 _____ Transcribe information from recording tape or stenograph machine notes.

Template F.1 (Continued)

16 _____ Take shorthand in meetings, conferences or from phone calls to produce minutes, notes, and summary reports.

17 _____ Use shorthand to record dictation and work instructions given by supervisor.

18 _____ Transcribe shorthand or stenotype notes using a typewriter or personal computer.

Process Written Materials

19 _____ Check completed forms or correspondence for inaccuracies in spelling, punctuation, grammar, format, neatness, or general appearance.

20 _____ Compose correspondence requiring specific knowledge of methods, procedures, policies, or other information.

21 _____ Produce copies of correspondence, reports, or other numerical or verbal data using a computer, copier, or printing equipment and prepare them for distribution.

22 _____ Forward completed correspondence or business files to supervisor for final review and approval.

23 _____ Prepare material for distribution using machine or by hand, copy, gather, fold, staple, or seal packets/envelopes.

Compute, Verify, and Record

24 _____ Maintain checklists, logs, worksheets, or other records used to monitor the status of a project or business activity.

25 _____ Perform calculations following a multi-step formula or procedure.

26 _____ Develop forms for the recording of numerical and statistical information.

27 _____ Verify accuracy and completeness of forms or records by comparing against original documents, items, master forms, or other standards.

28 _____ Compute statistics, such as means, medians, percentages, proportions, etc., using a calculator.

29 _____ Monitor expenditures against budget and/or contract specifications.

30 _____ Determine interest, adjustments, refunds, taxes, accrual figures, required balances, etc., or balance/reconcile records by performing calculations by hand or using a calculator.

Template F.1 (Continued)

Analyze, Interpret, and Report

31 _____ Prepare reports, based on information at hand, following standard procedures.

32 _____ Prepare reports requiring the investigation of various sources of information and systematic organization and presentation.

33 _____ Evaluate information requirements for financial report preparation.

34 _____ Maintain custody of evidence presented at meetings (including written memoranda, documents, etc.) for incorporation into transcript and records.

35 _____ Prepare analyses or summaries of programs, reports, specific operational items, or other data.

36 _____ Prepare displays (tables, graphs, charts, or diagrams) summarizing numerical or statistical data (e.g., financial data or operating statistics).

37 _____ Locate and retrieve data, records, or other information needed to conduct and/or complete work activities/transactions by conducting a search or investigation.

Bookkeeping

38 _____ Review accounting statements, expense reports, and standard forms for accuracy, completeness, and conformity to procedures.

39 _____ Locate sources of errors revealed through trial balance or failure to balance to an established control figure by comparing two or more sources.

40 _____ Allocate debits, credits, costs, charges, or other similar bookkeeping items of operational procedures to correct accounts or classification.

41 _____ Post entries in financial journals, ledgers, or other financial records.

42 _____ Reconcile out of balance journal or ledger or correct numerical figures by making necessary entries or adjustments.

43 _____ Verify and process invoices for payment.

44 _____ Assist in internal and external audits of fiscal and financial operations.

45 _____ Assist individuals with account problems by reviewing account information.

Template F.1 (Continued)

46 _____ Take a trial balance of accounts and locate and correct errors.

Code and Transcribe Data

47 _____ Prepare summary or data-entry/coding sheets for computer processing from information contained in other sources.

48 _____ Allocate charges or payments to individual departments and accounts using accounting codes.

49 _____ Verify accuracy of data coding and make necessary corrections.

50 _____ Code materials using number or letter codes.

51 _____ Make out various routine forms such as checks, receipts, invoices, form letter addresses, tine or cash reports, etc., according to standard operating procedure.

Data Entry

52 _____ Operate computer peripheral equipment (e.g., printer, forms buster, or magnetic tape units).

53 _____ Verify the accuracy of data entered into computer file using printout or visual screen.

54 _____ Select appropriate recording or transcribing programs based on the format of the coded data to be entered on data-keying terminal.

55 _____ Operate computer or data-entry terminals to enter, change, or establish information files.

56 _____ Analyze computer or computer equipment operation in relation to conditions displayed on screens, monitors, etc.

Receive and Distribute Mail

57 _____ Certify, register, insure, or complete forms associated with special mail services such as overnight courier or registered mail.

58 _____ Arrange for the delivery of confidential documents via courier or special messenger.

59 _____ Deliver mail, materials, or supplies to appropriate individuals.

60 _____ Distribute mail, bulletins, memos, and reports to employees and offices.

61 _____ Sort incoming and outgoing mail.

Reception Functions

62 _____ Greet visitors and direct them to the appropriate individual.

Template F.1 (Continued)

63 _____ Answer questions and give requested directions or other information directly or by telephone.

64 _____ Verify or confirm the identity of phone callers prior to initiating actions.

65 _____ Receive orders, requests, instructions, or information, personally or by telephone.

66 _____ Sign or initial documents to acknowledge receipt of valuables.

67 _____ Schedule use of facilities and/or equipment and assist individuals in their use.

68 _____ Serve as switchboard operator and answer telephone, relay messages, and provide routine information.

69 _____ Monitor remote TV camera screens to inspect approaching visitors to detect atypical or suspicious vehicle, activity, or events that occur in a monitored region.

Communications

70 _____ Select, assemble, and arrange distribution of news articles or other materials (brochures, leaflets, etc.) of interest within the organization.

71 _____ Assist in planning, coordinating and administering sponsored activities for employees or visitors (e.g., meetings, banquets).

72 _____ Provide information to employees on the availability and terms of company benefits and services.

73 _____ Assist employees in obtaining benefits or services.

74 _____ Maintain bulletin board or other displays of employee-relevant information.

75 _____ Keep a log of all events occurring during shift and make entries to journal to inform next shift personnel.

76 _____ Perform check of communications equipment and channels to ensure that they are in working order.

77 _____ Operate a dispatch radio to communicate with mobile units and personnel with hand-held radios.

Organizing and Scheduling Work

78 _____ Assign individuals to specific duties and locations and direct individuals in the performance of their assigned duties.

Template F.1 (Continued)

79 _____ Estimate materials, labor, and time requirements for specific projects.

80 _____ Set completion dates for forms, records, or reports.

81 _____ Inform individuals about work methods, objectives, progress, and expected changes.

82 _____ Distribute work assignments based on workload, work priorities, and worker capabilities.

83 _____ Develop and maintain up-to-date manuals of department/job practices and procedures to standardize the activities of subordinates.

84 _____ Develop sequenced action plans to correct problems with equipment or work processes or procedures.

85 _____ Identify productivity or quality deviations and determine cause by analyzing work or production records and take corrective action.

86 _____ Coordinate multiple and/or competing activities and assignments for efficient use of time and resources.

87 _____ Maintain a data base on a computer for financial data, inventory, personnel records, or government activity/decisions by entering new data, updates, or corrections as received.

88 _____ Prepare a roster of individuals' daily shift assignments by unit for use in tracking individuals by activity.

89 _____ Review information from outgoing shift personnel to determine priority of items for attention.

90 _____ Analyze information received from coworkers to determine the operations/work requirements, priority, and specific directions for assignments.

Operate and Maintain Equipment

91 _____ Determine need for equipment maintenance by conducting scheduled inspections.

92 _____ Arrange maintenance work for office equipment according to an established schedule or priority system.

93 _____ Repair, adjust, clean, and otherwise service electrical and mechanical office machines.

94 _____ Operate printing and microfilming equipment.

95 _____ Operate packaging and mailing equipment.

Template F.1 (Continued)

96 _____ Prepare and distribute/assign work orders for maintenance and repair of facility, utilities, equipment, or grounds.

Administrative Functions

97 _____ Notify or remind certain individuals or departments of meetings, scheduled dates, specific duties, or occurrences.

98 _____ Maintain an appointment book or schedule for one's supervisor.

99 _____ Coordinate the scheduling of meetings, facilities (conference rooms, etc.), or events (tours, banquets, classes, etc.) with other individuals or groups.

100 _____ Investigate the source of discrepancies in documentation or search for lost documents through coordination with others outside the department.

101 _____ Prepare expense vouchers and travel authorization and complete travel or meeting arrangements for departmental personnel.

102 _____ Prepare reports requiring the investigation of various sources of information and systematic organization and presentation.

103 _____ Draw up contracts, specifications, or other forms requiring specific knowledge of methods, procedures, policies, or other information.

Importance Ratings: Competencies

On the following pages you are to rate the importance of each job requirement. Importance should be judged in terms of how necessary this knowledge, skill, or ability is in order to do the job at a fully effective level of performance. For each requirement statement, proceed in two steps.

1. Consider whether or not the identified competency, that is, knowledge, skill, or ability, is necessary for effective performance of this job. If it is not required at all, you should rate the item a "0."

2. If the identified competency *is* required, then decide how important that competency is to fully effective job performance.

Use the following scale to make your judgments:

0   This rating indicates that this competency is not necessary for job performance.

1   This rating indicates that this competency has only minor or incidental importance for effective job performance. It is not essential to doing the job, but may occasionally be useful for doing some minor part of the job.

2   This rating indicates that this competency is desirable and useful for doing some minor part of the job but is not important to successfully meeting the major demands of the job.

3   This rating indicates that this competence is moderately important to successful job performance.

4   This rating indicates that this competence is very important to successful job performance.

This rating indicates that this competence is critically important for successful job performance.

Template F.2 Clerical/Administrative Services Importance Ratings: Competencies

Language Skills

1 _____ Ability to explain and demonstrate work procedures to others.

2 _____ Ability to use information coming from two or more sources, such as paying attention to a customer's conversation while listening for sounds from scanner.

3 _____ Ability to understand the spoken English language in individual words and sentences, to understand a co-worker's request or instruction.

4 _____ Ability to use spoken language to communicate information or ideas to answer a co-worker's questions or requests.

5 _____ Ability to coordinate work with co-workers through conversation/discussion wherein effectiveness depends on understanding others.

6 _____ Ability to understand spoken instructions or work procedures provided by supervisor or others.

7 _____ Ability to participate in group meetings or training sessions when effectiveness depends on understanding others.

8 _____ Ability to identify the important points of information from spoken content.

9 _____ Ability to provide routine spoken status reports or progress reports to supervisor or others in person, by telephone, or by radio.

10 _____ Ability to make informal reports or presentations to small groups.

11 _____ Ability to obtain information through personal interviews or personal conversations.

12 _____ Knowledge of what information should be considered confidential.

Calculating Skills

13 _____ Ability to accurately recognize and recall a series of numbers (e.g., telephone numbers, zip codes, or account codes).

14 _____ Ability to compare objects, letters, symbols, and numbers to determine identity or degree of similarity.

15 _____ Skill in following procedures to count money and make change for cash transactions.

Template F.2 (Continued)

16 _____ Ability to transcribe numerical information from one document to another.

17 _____ Ability to detect and correct arithmetic errors.

18 _____ Ability to detect errors or discrepancies in the entry of records, posting data, or other log entries.

19 _____ Skill in use of a calculator to perform arithmetic operations.

20 _____ Ability to perform a series of arithmetic operations, involving a multi-step formulas that include constant multipliers and use of memory functions using a multi-function calculator.

21 _____ Ability to perform simple arithmetic calculations (adding, subtracting, multiplying, dividing).

22 _____ Ability to perform calculations, involving algebraic formulas, statistical formulas, or complex procedures used in handling business data.

23 _____ Knowledge of forecasting or explanatory financial data analysis strategies (e.g., performance ratios, trend line analysis, value index equations, etc.).

Reading Skills

24 _____ Ability to read simple instructions or information, such as work orders, work assignments, CRT screen instructions, or descriptive material on containers.

25 _____ Ability to read detailed instructions or information, such as maintenance manuals, equipment information, or trade textbooks in order to troubleshoot/service/repair equipment.

26 _____ Ability to read complex material, such as technical handbooks, specifications and standards, or technical literature.

27 _____ Ability to read and comprehend professional journals and legal publications and to apply concepts, policies, and procedures to work activities.

28 _____ Ability to read computer printouts or other numerical material.

29 _____ Ability to read and interpret computer language, such as commands, codes, and instructions.

30 _____ Ability to follow established sequence of written procedures for start-up and operation of various types of production equipment.

Template F.2 (Continued)

Write and Process Written Materials

31 _____ Ability to enter simple information on forms or to otherwise record data according to standardized instructions, such as recording dates, codes, quantity, or number of errors.

32 _____ Ability to prepare simple records, such as work reports, inventory data, or information for next shift.

33 _____ Ability to prepare written records, such as equipment malfunction, performance results, or accident data.

34 _____ Ability to prepare detailed memoranda or reports, such as summary reports or project results.

35 _____ Ability to combine information from multiple sources into a final report.

36 _____ Knowledge of rules of grammar and punctuation.

37 _____ Ability to detect errors in grammar or punctuation or omissions through proofing letters, reports, forms, tables, or codes.

38 _____ Ability to spell commonly used English words and business and legal terms.

39 _____ Skill in typing from manuscript, draft copies, voice recordings, or dictation.

40 _____ Skill in operating word processing equipment (e.g., electric typewriter, or desk-top computer).

41 _____ Skill in recording dictation of letters or memos using shorthand, speed writing, or stenographic machine.

42 _____ Skill in recording the proceedings or minutes of meetings or conferences with multiple speakers using shorthand, speed writing, or stenotype machine.

Communication Skills

43 _____ Ability to convey information in a concise fashion without loss of necessary detail.

44 _____ Ability to organize information in reports, correspondence, etc., in a logical and meaningful manner.

45 _____ Ability to maintain or project a positive image in face-to-face conversations as well as in telephone conversations.

Template F.2 (Continued)

46 _____ Ability to calmly, politely, and firmly handle unsolicited communications from disturbed individuals.

47 _____ Knowledge of standard procedures used to respond and direct 911 calls.

48 _____ Skill in eliciting information from excited or distressed individuals who are 911 callers.

49 _____ Knowledge of NCIC procedures, codes, and methods for data entry, modification, update, and cancellation.

50 _____ Ability to memorize phone numbers and names of persons to call quickly in the event of an emergency.

51 _____ Ability to respond to multiple, simultaneous communication room signals requiring quick reactions.

52 _____ Knowledge of radio communications terminology and 10-code system.

Personal Relations and Teamwork Skills

53 _____ Knowledge of norms of courtesy and etiquette in relation with the public and co-workers.

54 _____ Skill in expressing apologies or explanations for the inconveniences of others.

55 _____ Ability to negotiate priorities with individuals in the organization.

56 _____ Ability to predict the reactions of others to information, events, or conditions.

57 _____ Skill in the application of timing, tact, and discretion in communicating business-related information.

58 _____ Ability to recognize and capitalize on social and interpersonal cues in dealing with others.

59 _____ Ability to focus attention on work assignments or responsibilities in a distracting environment.

60 _____ Knowledge of factors that have an effect on work assignments' completion time.

Work and Organization Skills

61 _____ Ability to adjust schedules to reflect changing situations, requirements, or priorities.

62 _____ Ability to work without close supervision.

Template F.2 (Continued)

63 _____ Ability to recognize the impact of what other employees are doing upon one's own area of responsibility.

64 _____ Ability to interpret and implement instructions issued by management.

65 _____ Ability to follow through on specific problems or programs and maintain a continuous level of emphasis until completion.

66 _____ Ability to work effectively with others in close or stressful situations.

67 _____ Ability to maintain complex clerical records and prepare reports from such records.

68 _____ Knowledge of standard office procedures and basic filing methods and materials.

Data-Entry Skills

69 _____ Skill in performing key entry of alpha or numeric material.

70 _____ Skill in entering numerical or coded data into computer using keyboard operations.

71 _____ Knowledge of data-entry operations with reference to speed and accuracy.

72 _____ Knowledge of procedures and codes used to enter, change, or delete computer data or information.

Computer Operation Skills

73 _____ Ability to operate computer text and data entry, retrieval terminals, and peripheral equipment.

74 _____ Knowledge of procedures and codes to enter, change, or delete computerized information.

75 _____ Skill in operating computer peripherals such as printers, tape and disc drives, etc.

76 _____ Ability to use packaged computer software programs to analyze business data or arrange business information.

77 _____ Knowledge of computer program or format required for use with various types of data.

Bookkeeping and Accounting Skills

78 _____ Knowledge of procedures used to credit or debit accounts based on activity in area of responsibility.

Template F.2 (Continued)

79 _____ Knowledge of procedures used to post general-ledger entries.

80 _____ Ability to detect errors or discrepancies in the entry of records, posting data, or other log entries.

81 _____ Knowledge of procedures used to calculate principle, interest, taxes, fees, discount ,and payment schedules.

82 _____ Knowledge of standard bookkeeping and accounting principles and procedures.

83 _____ Knowledge of procedures for handling time cards and preparing payroll records and documentation.

84 _____ Skill in accurately making cash transactions to include making change for cash payments.

85 _____ Ability to process large sums of money and make a variety of cost computations.

Supervisory Skills

86 _____ Ability to distinguish between effective and ineffective procedures or job performance.

87 _____ Ability to evaluate and give others feedback on their job performance.

88 _____ Ability to communicate evaluative judgments and descriptive comments of on-the-job performance of subordinates.

89 _____ Ability to coach subordinates to correct ineffective work practices or to remedy performance deficiencies.

90 _____ Ability to explain or demonstrate work techniques, safety procedures, etc., to others.

91 _____ Ability to identify strengths and weaknesses of subordinate performance and to establish plans for training and development.

92 _____ Ability to apply personnel rules in a fair and consistent manner.

93 _____ Ability to evaluate relevant applicant background and job skills through review of resumes and application forms or through personal interviews.

94 _____ Ability to assess the capabilities and limitations of individuals in order to allocate personnel or make job assignments.

95 _____ Skill in identifying the relevant facts underlying conflicting claims or issues.

Template F.2 (Continued)

Scheduling and Coordinating

96 _____ Ability to break down a complex situation into its primary components.

97 _____ Skill in making the arrangements, scheduling, and completing other details for meetings.

98 _____ Ability to coordinate the activities of other individuals or departments on joint projects.

99 _____ Ability to evaluate and to establish project priorities based on relative merits, demands, or requirements.

100 _____ Ability to plan and conduct multiple activities within a specified time frame to ensure goal or deadline achievement.

101 _____ Ability to evaluate and choose between conflicting alternatives based on partial or incomplete information.

102 _____ Ability to adjust project schedules or work assignments in response to changes in conditions or priorities.

Work and Organization Adaptation

103 _____ Knowledge of the protocol regarding meetings, conferences, events, appointments, and authority relationships.

104 _____ Knowledge of the restrictions and proprietary standards regarding discussion of organization operations, plans, problems, or relationships with other organizations.

105 _____ Knowledge of personal standards regarding dress, language, personal hygiene, attendance, and expressed attitudes toward co-workers or people associated with the organization.

106 _____ Ability to distinguish between problems that can be resolved through routine procedures from those that require specialized response or attention of other persons.

107 _____ Ability to identify, accommodate, and adapt to the conditions and circumstances of the work, the organization, rules and regulations, and relationships with other people to maintain a smooth-running and efficient organization.

108 _____ Ability to maintain attention and pace of work activities when performing repetitive tasks or when confronted by distractions, competing requirements, or persons.

Appendix G

PROFESSIONAL ADMINISTRATIVE JOB ANALYSIS TEMPLATES

1. Name of Analyst:_____

2. Location:_____

3. Analyst's Job Title:_____

4. Time in present position (years):_____ (months):_____

5. Time with company (years):_____ (months):_____

This procedure is designed to identify those job activities and competencies most important for professional administrative jobs. The information from these templates will be used to conduct a job-related selection assessment for this position.

There are two templates. Template G.1 consists of a list of activities that may or may not be an important part of the target job. You will be asked to rate each statement as to that activity's importance for the job. On the next page there is a rating scale and a brief explanation of how to use it.

Template G.2 contains a list of competencies statements. The focus of that template is to determine which competencies are necessary for doing this job successfully. Specific instructions for rating these requirement statements appear with the template.

The key points you should keep in mind as you go through this template are

1. Your judgment and your ratings are to be based on the job as it is now actually performed, not as it might ideally be done.

2. Your judgment should be your own independent judgment. Do not ask anyone else how you should rate an item. Whether it is judged to be important or not is your decision, not anyone else's.

3. If you simply cannot make an honest, accurate rating, leave the item blank.

Importance Ratings: Work Activities

In this section, you are to rate the importance of different work activities with respect to this job. For each statement, proceed in two steps.

1. Consider whether a work activity is or is not part of the job. If it is not part of the job, rate the task "0."

2. If the activity is one that is done by an individual in the job, decide how important it is in that job. Consider the activity in terms of its importance for fully effective job performance.

Use the following scale to make your judgments:

0   This rating indicates that the work activity is never done and is not part of the job.

1   This rating indicates that the work activity has only minor importance relative to other activities performed by individuals in this job. Considering all activities, it would have the lowest priority or importance.

2   This rating indicates that the work activity has a relatively low level of importance compared to other job activities.

3   This rating indicates that the work activity is moderately important for fully effective job performance relative to other activities, and has about average priority among all activities performed.

4   This rating indicates that the work activity is very important to fully effective job performance. It has a higher degree of importance or priority than most other activities.

5   This rating indicates that the work activity is one of the few most essential activities performed. It is one of the most critical aspects of the job.

Template G.1 Professional Administrative Importance Ratings: Work Activities

Process Written Materials

1 _____ Check completed forms or correspondence for inaccuracies in spelling, punctuation, grammar, format, neatness, or general appearance.

2 _____ Compose correspondence requiring specific knowledge of methods, procedures, policies, or other information.

3 _____ Prepare tables, graphs, charts, etc., based on data from other sources.

4 _____ Compose letters, memos, or other documents for the supervisor's signature from notes or following general instructions.

5 _____ Prepare drafts and final copy of legal documents, contracts, letters, etc.

6 _____ Prepare letters, memos, reports, or other documents from rough draft.

7 _____ Forward completed correspondence or business files to supervisor for final review and approval.

8 _____ Prepare packages of material for distribution.

File and Retrieve Materials

9 _____ Review, update, or revise file contents to reflect current status of subject.

10 _____ Search indices, manuals, files, records, or other sources for desired or missing information on specific subjects.

11 _____ Maintain records of incoming and outgoing materials through use of catalogues, computerized circulation system, or withdrawal file.

12 _____ Retrieve records and/or information from file and forward to others.

Compute, Verify, Record

13 _____ Maintain checklists, logs, worksheets, or other records used to monitor the status of a project or business activity.

14 _____ Develop forms for the recording of numerical and statistical information.

15 _____ Take notes in meetings, conferences, or from phone calls to produce minutes, notes, or summary reports.

16 _____ Verify accuracy and completeness of forms or records by comparing against original documents, items, master forms, or other standards.

17 _____ Compute statistics, such as means, medians, percentages, proportions, etc.

18 _____ Monitor expenditures against budget and/or contract specifications.

Template G.1 (Continued)

19 _____ Determine interest, adjustments, refunds, taxes, accrual figures, required balances, etc., or balance/reconcile records.

Analyze, Interpret, Report

20 _____ Prepare reports based on information at hand following standard procedures.

21 _____ Prepare reports requiring the investigation of various sources of information and systematic organization for presentation.

22 _____ Evaluate information requirements or developing financial reports.

23 _____ Maintain custody of evidence presented at meetings (including written memoranda, documents, etc.) for incorporation into transcripts and records.

24 _____ Prepare analyses or summaries of programs, reports, specific operational items, or other data.

25 _____ Prepare displays (tables, graphs, charts, or diagrams) summarizing numerical data (e.g., financial data or operating statistics).

26 _____ Locate and retrieve data, records, or other information needed to conduct and/or complete work activities/transactions by conducting a search or investigation.

Keep Books

27 _____ Review accounting statements, expense reports, and standard forms for accuracy, completeness, and conformity to procedures.

28 _____ Allocate debits, credits, costs, charges, or other similar bookkeeping items of operational procedures to correct accounts or classification.

29 _____ Post entries in financial journals, ledgers, or other financial records.

30 _____ Reconcile out of balance journal or ledger or correct numerical figures by making necessary entries or adjustments.

31 _____ Verify and process invoices for payment.

32 _____ Assist in internal and external audits of fiscal and financial operations.

33 _____ Assist individuals with account problems by reviewing account information.

34 _____ Construct a trial balance of accounts and locate and correct errors.

Communicate

35 _____ Select, assemble, and arrange distribution of news articles or other materials of interest within the organization.

(continues)

Template G.1 (Continued)

36 _____ Assist in planning, coordinating, and administering sponsored activities for employees or visitors (e.g., meetings or banquets).

37 _____ Provide information to employees on the availability and terms of company benefits and services.

38 _____ Research and write technical reports for others of comparable background and knowledge.

39 _____ Research and write reports presenting technical information to an audience with less knowledge of the subject.

40 _____ Represent the company to outside audiences.

41 _____ Create and distribute a regular company newsletter for all staff.

42 _____ Prepare formal policy statements or reports for either internal or external distribution.

Supervise

43 _____ Plan and coordinate the assignment or execution of duties performed by other individuals.

44 _____ Evaluate the work performance of individuals according to established performance standards and give feedback to correct deficiencies.

45 _____ Intervene to resolve disagreements or interpersonal difficulties among employees.

46 _____ Inform individuals about work methods, objectives, progress, and expected changes.

47 _____ Distribute work assignments based on workload, work priorities, and worker capabilities.

48 _____ Evaluate effects of employee training by observing and monitoring employee job behavior.

49 _____ Establish and communicate performance goals and standards to subordinates to clarify job and organizational expectations and requirements.

50 _____ Review staff assignments to ensure appropriate and equitable assignments are maintained.

51 _____ Assign subordinates to projects based on project objectives, methods, or subject area and on the subordinates' interests, job skills, and developmental needs.

52 _____ Identify subordinates with personal problems that affect job performance and refer to resource agency.

Template G.1 (Continued)

53 _____ Counsel employees on career development opportunities, training needs, and their individual development plans.

54 _____ Counsel employees whose work performance is below standard or who have been disciplined due to violation of company policy.

Plan, Organize, Schedule, Coordinate

55 _____ Assign individuals to specific duties and locations and direct individuals in the performance of their assigned duties.

56 _____ Set completion dates for forms, records, or reports.

57 _____ Inform individuals about work methods, objectives, progress, and expected changes.

58 _____ Distribute work assignments based on workload, work priorities, and worker capabilities.

59 _____ Develop and maintain up-to-date manuals of department/job practices and procedures to standardize the activities of subordinates.

60 _____ Develop sequenced action plans to correct problems with equipment or work processes or procedures.

61 _____ Coordinate multiple and/or competing activities and assignments for efficient use of time and resources.

62 _____ Maintain and keep up-to-date database on a computer for financial data, inventory, personnel records, etc.

Perform Administrative Functions

63 _____ Maintain an appointment book or schedule for one's supervisor.

64 _____ Coordinate the scheduling of meetings, facilities (conference rooms, etc.), or events (tours, banquets, classes, etc.) with other individuals or groups.

65 _____ Investigate the source of discrepancies in documentation or search for missing documents through coordination with others outside the department.

66 _____ Prepare and present reports requiring the investigation of various sources of information and systematic organization.

67 _____ Draw up contracts, specifications, or other forms requiring specific knowledge of methods, procedures, policies, or other information.

Importance Ratings: Competencies

On the following pages you are to rate the importance of each job requirement. Importance should be judged in terms of how necessary this knowledge, skill, or ability is in order to do the job at a fully effective level of performance. For each requirement statement, proceed in two steps.

1. Consider whether or not the identified competency, that is, knowledge, skill, or ability, is necessary for effective performance of this job. If it is not required at all, you should rate the item a "0."

2. If the identified competency *is* required, then decide how important that competency is to fully effective job performance.

Use the following scale to make your judgments:

0   This rating indicates that this competency is not necessary for job performance.

1   This rating indicates that this competency has only minor or incidental importance for effective job performance. It is not essential to doing the job, but may occasionally be useful for doing some minor part of the job.

2   This rating indicates that this competency is desirable and useful for doing some minor part of the job but is not important to successfully meeting the major demands of the job.

3   This rating indicates that this competence is moderately important to successful job performance.

4   This rating indicates that this competence is very important to successful job performance.

This rating indicates that this competence is critically important for successful job performance.

Template G.2 Professional Administrative Importance Ratings: Competencies

Analyze and Evaluate

1 _____ Ability to formulate research designs and statistical strategies that will provide information relevant to specific hypotheses or research problems.

2 _____ Ability to use financial data to develop projected profit-and-loss and return-on-investment information.

3 _____ Ability to perform calculations involving algebraic or statistical formulas or other procedures used in handling business data.

4 _____ Ability to recognize when significant new information calls into question a previously determined solution to a problem so that additional analysis is required.

5 _____ Ability to identify and use temporary solutions that can mitigate an existing risk or problem until a permanent solution can be found.

6 _____ Ability to assess and evaluate changes in individual behavior necessary to respond to planned interventions.

7 _____ Ability to evaluate and integrate data from multiple sources to reach a conclusion and formulate recommendations.

8 _____ Ability to analyze and categorize information gathered through interviews or surveys.

Research and Investigate

9 _____ Ability to identify the relevant facts underlying conflicting claims or issues.

10 _____ Ability to recognize what additional information about a problem situation should be collected.

11 _____ Ability to take various points of view in analyzing, interpreting, and evaluating data.

12 _____ Knowledge of principles and techniques of how to present oneself and conduct a meeting to establish trust and obtain emotionally charged information.

Apply Legal and Regulatory Knowledge

13 _____ Knowledge of the characteristics of an interview or investigation that may be interpreted as intrusion, invasion of privacy, violation of rights, confidentiality, and, thus, vulnerable to legal challenge.

(continues)

Template G.2 (Continued)

14 _____ Knowledge of the features and characteristics of state and federal regulations or laws regarding assigned area of professional responsibility.

Access and Use Computer Systems and Resources

15 _____ Knowledge of database, accounting, word processing, or other computer programs as necessary.

16 _____ Knowledge of information contained in various databases or other programs related to professional area of responsibility

17 _____ Ability to access various databases, online sources, etc., to obtain relevant information.

Plan, Organize, Schedule, Coordinate

18 _____ Ability to determine proper priority and perspective when handling multiple activities or projects.

19 _____ Ability to determine when, where, and how to establish and maintain management controls to monitor individual or team activities.

20 _____ Ability to calculate manpower, materials, and other resource requirements for completion of activities or projects.

21 _____ Ability to determine the sequence in which component parts or steps of a project or activity must be conducted.

22 _____ Ability to formulate long-range programmatic plans to address significant issues or goals using systematic, formal methods such as PERT, etc.

23 _____ Ability to identify the key decision points and milestones in the planning, implementation, and control of a project.

24 _____ Knowledge of the significant factors to be considered and how to weigh them when making strategic organizational decisions.

25 _____ Knowledge of activities of competitors and trends that could create future opportunities or problems.

Supervise

26 _____ Ability to disregard one's personal feelings in the assignment of tasks or in the conduct of business activities.

27 _____ Ability to explain or demonstrate work techniques to subordinates and provide them with feedback on their performance.

Template G.2 (Continued)

28 _____ Ability to evaluate the performance of subordinates in terms of organizational requirements and standards.

29 _____ Ability to recognize situational constraints or conditions that affect supervisory behavior or style.

30 _____ Ability to evaluate and give others feedback on job performance.

31 _____ Ability to communicate evaluative judgments and descriptive comments on the job performance of subordinates.

32 _____ Ability to coach subordinates to correct ineffective work practices or to remedy performance deficiencies.

33 _____ Ability to identify strengths and weaknesses of subordinate performance and establish plans for training and development.

34 _____ Ability to apply personnel rules in a fair and consistent manner.

35 _____ Ability to evaluate relevant applicant background and job skills through review of resumes and application forms or through personal interviews.

36 _____ Ability to assess the capabilities and limitations of individuals in order to allocate personnel or make job assignments.

Manage Operations

37 _____ Ability to adjust one's pace of activity to keep up with rapidly occurring events or changing conditions and circumstances and meet important management requirements.

38 _____ Ability to identify and prioritize requirements of ongoing operations or projects in order to maintain management control and achieve the desired outcomes.

39 _____ Skill in selecting standard solutions to problems or in modifying standard operating procedures to make things work when unanticipated, novel, or unique developments occur.

40 _____ Ability to identify obstacles to the flow of an activity and to identify and initiate alternative procedures to maintain continuity of the activity.

Communicate Verbally and in Writing

41 _____ Ability to phrase and sequence questions to obtain information or clarify issues in interviews and/or informal conversations.

(continues)

Template G.2 (Continued)

42 _____ Skill in differentiating real and relevant information from false and irrelevant content.

43 _____ Ability to design a presentation that addresses the interests of the listeners and takes into account their level of understanding of the subject.

44 _____ Ability to prepare, present, and defend a proposal in a constructive and persuasive manner.

45 _____ Ability to review reports for quality using standards of logic, clarity, and adequacy of recommendations and supporting arguments

46 _____ Ability to prepare technical reports for use by others with comparable background.

47 _____ Ability to communicate company policy or intent in contracts, letters, or other formal documents.

48 _____ Ability to read and comprehend professional journals and legal publications and to apply concepts, policies, and procedures to work activities.

Manage Personal/Interpersonal Relations

49 _____ Ability to ignore personal likes and dislikes in business dealings and focus on the desired outcomes.

50 _____ Ability to recognize social and interpersonal cues in dealing with others and to utilize them to realize organizational goals.

51 _____ Ability to build and maintain credibility in organizational relations with others.

52 _____ Ability to provide criticism or objections to the views of another in a way that avoids personal accusations or acrimony.

Make Choices and Solve Problems

53 _____ Ability to recognize problems early and to take prompt action to resolve them while still small.

54 _____ Ability to make choices or decisions affecting the security or well-being of others and/or which involve serious risks or consequences.

55 _____ Ability to distinguish between symptoms and causes of problems.

56 _____ Ability to recognize when and to specify what additional information is necessary to solve problems.

Template G.2 (Continued)

57 _____ Ability to specify a sequence of activities to locate or retrieve lost or misplaced files, documents, etc.

58 _____ Ability to recognize what specific additional information about a problem or situation should be collected.

Adapt to Work and Organization Requirements

59 _____ Knowledge of organizational practices and norms regarding meetings, events, appointments, authority relationships, and organizational structure.

60 _____ Knowledge of the relationships, dependencies, and contingencies among organizational units, key management positions, and other positions and functions.

61 _____ Knowledge of the standards regarding discussion of company operations, plans, problems, and business and professional relations with other organizations.

62 _____ Knowledge of the standards regarding dress, language, personal hygiene, attendance, and expressed attitudes when identified with the organization.

Appendix H

SUPERVISOR/FIRST-LINE MANAGER JOB ANALYSIS TEMPLATE

1. Name of Analyst:_____

2. Location:_____

3. Analyst's Job Title:_____

4. Time in present position (years):_____ (months):_____

5. Time with company (years):_____ (months):_____

This procedure is designed to identify those job activities and competencies most important for supervisory and first-line management jobs. The information from this template will be used to conduct a job-related selection assessment for this position.

There are two templates. Template H.1 consists of a list of activities that may or may not be an important part of the target job. You will be asked to rate each statement as to that activity's importance for the job. On the next page there is a rating scale and a brief explanation of how to use it.

Template H.2 contains a list of competencies statements. The focus of that part is to determine which competencies are necessary for doing this job successfully. Specific instructions for rating these requirement statements appear following the instructions for rating the job activities.

The key points you should keep in mind as you go through this template are

1. Your judgment and your ratings are to be based on the job as it is now actually performed, not as it might ideally be done.

2. Your judgment should be your own independent judgment. Do not ask anyone else how you should rate an item. Whether it is judged to be important or not is your decision, not anyone else's.

3. If you simply cannot make an honest, accurate rating, leave the item blank.

Importance Ratings: Work Activities

In this section, you are to rate the importance of different work activities with respect to this job. For each statement, proceed in two steps.

1. Consider whether a work activity is or is not part of the job. If it is not part of the job, rate the task "0."

2. If the activity is one that is done by an individual in the job, decide how important it is in that job. Consider the activity in terms of its importance for fully effective job performance.

Use the following scale to make your judgments:

0   This rating indicates that the work activity is never done and is not part of the job.

1   This rating indicates that the work activity has only minor importance relative to other activities performed by individuals in this job. Considering all activities, it would have the lowest priority or importance.

2   This rating indicates that the work activity has a relatively low level of importance compared to other job activities.

3   This rating indicates that the work activity is moderately important for fully effective job performance relative to other activities, and has about average priority among all activities performed.

4   This rating indicates that the work activity is very important to fully effective job performance. It has a higher degree of importance or priority than most other activities.

5   This rating indicates that the work activity is one of the few most essential activities performed. It is one of the most critical aspects of the job.

Template H.1 Supervisor/First-Line Manager Importance Ratings: Work Activities

Supervise and Manage Performance Quality

1 _____ Review subordinates' work and provide action-oriented feedback and mentoring to improve performance and correct deficiencies.

2 _____ Refer a subordinate whose personal problems affect job performance to EAP or other appropriate resource for assistance.

3 _____ Conduct training programs and mentor to encourage employees to develop their technical, supervisory, or professional skills.

4 _____ Evaluate a subordinate's performance against established guidelines, objectives, and performance standards.

5 _____ Identify employee training needs based on business activities and plans and evaluation of employee job skills.

6 _____ Conduct and document employee disciplinary interviews.

7 _____ Inform subordinates about work methods, objectives, progress, and expected changes.

8 _____ Mentor subordinates and support their contributions and high-quality performance through words of encouragement, praise, direct assistance, etc.

9 _____ Implement organizational policies and procedures and product or service standards as established by management.

10 _____ Discuss job performance problems with subordinates in order to identify issues and causes and to develop solutions.

11 _____ Ensure that subordinates adhere to proper procedures and quality standards, meet deadlines, and correct errors or problems.

12 _____ Ensure that subordinates understand and follow safety, sanitation, or other related regulations.

13 _____ Observe work and monitor gauges, screens, or other indicators to ensure adherence to production or processing standards.

Manage Human Resources

14 _____ Encourage subordinates to work together to accomplish tasks.

15 _____ Develop training programs, personally or with HRD specialists, to introduce new technology or procedures.

Template H.1 (Continued)

16 _____ Implement work practices that promote cooperation and build mutual trust and respect among members of work groups.

17 _____ Make recommendations for pay adjustments for subordinates.

18 _____ Review manpower/personnel data to discern trends in absenteeism, tardiness, or turnover to facilitate development of personnel policies.

19 _____ Conduct exit interviews to determine causes for separation and to identify trends that have policy implications.

20 _____ Interview job candidates to determine qualifications and suitability for employment in specific positions.

21 _____ Develop and maintain up-to-date manuals of department/job practices and procedures to standardize the activities of subordinates.

22 _____ Distribute work assignments based on workload, work priorities, and worker competencies.

Analyze and Solve Problems

23 _____ Question employees to obtain diagnostic information for maintenance or repair of equipment.

24 _____ Develop sequenced action plans to rectify identified problems with equipment or production lines.

25 _____ Examine equipment to determine primary and/or contributory factors of equipment failure.

26 _____ Monitor in-progress products to identify potential problems or needed adjustments to production equipment or procedures.

27 _____ Analyze work or production records to examine productivity or quality issues and determine cause and take corrective action.

28 _____ Provide subordinates with guidance in handling difficult or complex problems and in resolving escalated complaints or disputes.

Plan, Organize, Schedule, Coordinate

29 _____ Establish production schedules and allocate direct labor to achieve and maintain production line balance and product flow.

30 _____ Determine changes in equipment layout and staffing in response to changes in product mix.

(continues)

Template H.1 (Continued)

31 _____ Adjust work schedules or project priorities to meet emergencies or changing conditions.

32 _____ Coordinate multiple and/or competing activities and assignments for efficient use of time and resources.

33 _____ Evaluate the production schedule in order to anticipate required changes in personnel assignments.

34 _____ Confer with other supervisors to coordinate operations and activities within or between departments.

35 _____ Consider relative costs and benefits of alternative options to choose the most appropriate one.

Communicate

36 _____ Call and conduct staff meetings to exchange information, define objectives, establish priorities, and develop solutions for emerging problems.

37 _____ Obtain and/or clarify information from employees relevant to work procedures and standards.

38 _____ Present work-related information (such as work or safety procedures, policy changes, etc.) clearly and concisely.

39 _____ Prepare and submit reports (e.g., problems encountered, downtime, workload volume, maintenance activities, etc.) to management.

40 _____ Review technical reports or manufacturer notices concerning changes in equipment, parts, or operating procedures.

41 _____ Confer with appropriate individuals to resolve worker problems, complaints, or grievances.

42 _____ Respond to customers' questions and/or complaints about products, services, or policies and procedures.

Manage Personal/Interpersonal Relations

43 _____ Maintain composure and a productive level of effort in stressful situations.

44 _____ Develop and maintain constructive and cooperative working relationships with others.

45 _____ Intervene to resolve disagreements or interpersonal difficulties among employees.

Template H.1 (Continued)

46 _____ Identify situations that, if unchanged, could lead to conflict among employees.

47 _____ Investigate recurrent disputes among employees to determine causes and contributing factors.

48 _____ Review and evaluate employee relations activities to determine their effectiveness.

49 _____ Review local conditions or situations to predict labor relations problems.

Manage Work Unit

50 _____ Use computer systems and programs as required to fulfill job responsibilities.

51 _____ Inspect materials, equipment, products to detect malfunctions or defects.

52 _____ Manage time effectively.

53 _____ Read and analyze charts, work orders, production and shipping schedules, etc., to determine production requirements and to evaluate current production estimates and outputs.

54 _____ Monitor subordinates' work activities and productivity to ensure targets are realistically set and consistently met.

Importance Ratings: Competencies

On the following pages you are to rate the importance of each job requirement. Importance should be judged in terms of how necessary this knowledge, skill, or ability is in order to do the job at a fully effective level of performance. For each requirement statement, proceed in two steps.

1. Consider whether or not the identified competency, that is, knowledge, skill, or ability, is necessary for effective performance of this job. If it is not required at all, you should rate the item a "0."

2. If the identified competency *is* required, then decide how important that competency is to fully effective job performance.

Use the following scale to make your judgments:

0   This rating indicates that this competency is not necessary for job performance.

1   This rating indicates that this competency has only minor or incidental importance for effective job performance. It is not essential to doing the job, but may occasionally be useful for doing some minor part of the job.

2   This rating indicates that this competency is desirable and useful for doing some minor part of the job but is not important to successfully meeting the major demands of the job.

3   This rating indicates that this competence is moderately important to successful job performance.

4   This rating indicates that this competence is very important to successful job performance.

This rating indicates that this competence is critically important for successful job performance.

Template H.2 Supervisor/First-Line Manager Importance Ratings: Competencies

Supervise and Manage Performance

1 _____ Ability to distinguish between effective and ineffective procedures or job performance.

2 _____ Ability to communicate evaluative judgments and descriptive comments on the job performance of subordinates.

3 _____ Knowledge of alternative techniques and procedures for training and their relative advantages or disadvantages.

4 _____ Ability to coach subordinates to correct ineffective work practices or to remedy performance deficiencies.

5 _____ Ability to recognize and capitalize on situational restrictions or conditions that affect choice of supervisory style.

6 _____ Ability to recognize and deal with conditions that interfere with the performance of employees.

7 _____ Ability to react immediately and give precise instructions in emergency situations.

8 _____ Ability to assign tasks and delegate authority according to subordinates' capabilities and developmental needs.

9 _____ Ability to assess the morale of subordinates.

10 _____ Ability to enforce rules and regulations without alienating subordinates.

11 _____ Ability to apply personnel rules in a fair and consistent manner.

12 _____ Ability to assess the capabilities and limitations of individuals in order to allocate personnel or make job assignments.

13 _____ Skill in mentoring subordinates and guiding their career development.

14 _____ Knowledge of team-building techniques and skill in implementing them.

15 _____ Ability to encourage subordinates to identify common goals and cooperate to achieve them.

Plan, Organize, Schedule, Coordinate

16 _____ Knowledge of factors that have an effect upon work assignment completion time.

17 _____ Ability to coordinate the activities of other individuals or departments on joint projects.

(continues)

Template H.2 (Continued)

18 _____ Ability to schedule multiple projects that compete for limited resources (time, equipment, personnel, etc.).

19 _____ Ability to evaluate and to establish project priorities based on relative merits, demands, or requirements.

Organize and Use Information

20 _____ Skill in identifying the relevant facts underlying conflicting claims.

21 _____ Ability to take various points of view in analyzing, interpreting, and evaluating data.

22 _____ Ability to evaluate and choose between conflicting alternatives based on partial or incomplete information.

23 _____ Ability to locate and identify primary and/or contributory causes of production problems.

24 _____ Skill in obtaining information from subordinates about performance problems and issues and working with them to devise solutions.

25 _____ Ability to guide subordinates toward successful methods of handling difficult or complex problems and resolving escalated complaints or disputes.

Communicate

26 _____ Skill in soliciting information through interviews or conversation.

27 _____ Ability to convey information in a concise fashion without losing necessary detail.

28 _____ Ability to help others to clarify a confusing request, question, or response.

29 _____ Ability to translate informal conversation into action-oriented memoranda.

30 _____ Ability to prepare both routine and special reports for superiors (e.g., problems encountered, downtime, workload volume, maintenance activities, etc.).

31 _____ Ability to review relevant technical reports or manufacturer notices and disseminate this information to subordinates.

32 _____ Skill in working with other supervisors to coordinate operations and activities within and between departments.

Manage Personal/Interpersonal Relations

33 _____ Skill in using tact and discretion to communicate business-related information appropriately.

Template H.2 (Continued)

34 _____ Ability to recognize and address interpersonal problems that interfere with workgroup performance.

35 _____ Ability to recognize and capitalize on social and interpersonal cues in dealing with others.

36 _____ Ability to focus attention on work assignments or responsibilities in a distracting environment.

37 _____ Ability to identify and forestall potential sources of conflict among subordinates.

Manage Work Unit

38 _____ Knowledge of computer systems and programs needed to fulfill job responsibilities.

39 _____ Ability to manage time effectively.

40 _____ Ability to monitor subordinates' work activities and productivity to ensure that targets are realistically set and consistently met.

41 _____ Knowledge of materials, equipment, and products enabling identification of defects or malfunctions.

42 _____ Ability to read and analyze charts, production schedules, or targets, and so forth, to determine production requirements and to evaluate current production estimates and outputs.

Adapt to Work and Organization

43 _____ Knowledge of the protocol regarding meetings, conferences, events, appointments, and authority relationships.

44 _____ Knowledge of organizational standards regarding dress, language, personal hygiene, attendance, and expressed attitudes toward co-workers, customers/clients, or others.

45 _____ Ability to distinguish problems that can be resolved through routine procedures from those that require specialized response or attention of other persons.

46 _____ Ability to identify, accommodate, and adapt to the conditions and circumstances of the work, the organization, rules and regulations, and relationships with other people to maintain a smooth-running and efficient organization.

Appendix I

SENIOR MANAGEMENT/EXECUTIVE JOB ANALYSIS TEMPLATES

1. Name of Analyst:_____
2. Location:_____
3. Analyst's Job Title:_____
4. Time in present position (years):_____ (months):_____
5. Time with company (years):_____ (months):_____

   This procedure is designed to identify those job activities and competencies most important for senior-level management and executive jobs. The information from this template will be used to conduct a job-related selection assessment for this position.

   There are two templates. Template I.1 consists of a list of activities that may or may not be an important part of the target job. You will be asked to rate each statement as to that activity's importance for the job. On the next page there is a rating scale and a brief explanation of how to use it.

   Template I.2 contains a list of competency statements. The focus of that part is to determine which competencies are necessary for doing this job successfully. Specific instructions for rating these requirement statements appear following the instructions for rating the job activities.

The key points you should keep in mind as you go through this template are

1. Your judgment and your ratings are to be based on the job as it is now actually performed, not as it might ideally be done.

2. Your judgment should be your own independent judgment. Do not ask anyone else how you should rate an item. Whether it is judged to be important or not is your decision, not anyone else's.

3. If you simply cannot make an honest, accurate rating, leave the item blank.

In this section, you are to rate the importance of different work activities with respect to this job. For each statement, proceed in two steps.

1. Consider whether a work activity is or is not part of the job. If it is not part of the job, rate the task "0."
2. If the activity is one that is done by an individual in the job, decide how important it is in that job. Consider the activity in terms of its importance for fully effective job performance.

Use the following scale to make your judgments:

0   This rating indicates that the work activity is never done and is not part of the job.

1   This rating indicates that the work activity has only minor importance relative to other activities performed by individuals in this job. Considering all activities, it would have the lowest priority or importance.

2   This rating indicates that the work activity has a relatively low level of importance compared to other job activities.

3   This rating indicates that the work activity is moderately important for fully effective job performance relative to other activities, and has about average priority among all activities performed.

4   This rating indicates that the work activity is very important to fully effective job performance. It has a higher degree of importance or priority than most other activities.

5   This rating indicates that the work activity is one of the few most essential activities performed. It is one of the most critical aspects of the job.

Importance Ratings: Work Activities

On the following pages you are to rate the importance of each job requirement. Importance should be judged in terms of how necessary this knowledge, skill, or ability is in order to do the job at a fully effective level of performance. For each requirement statement, proceed in two steps.

1. Consider whether or not the identified competency, that is, knowledge, skill, or ability, is necessary for effective performance of this job. If it is not required at all, you should rate the item a "0."

2. If the identified competency *is* required, then decide how important that competency is to fully effective job performance.

   Use the following scale to make your judgments:

0   This rating indicates that this competency is not necessary for job performance.

1   This rating indicates that this competency has only minor or incidental importance for effective job performance. It is not essential to doing the job, but may occasionally be useful for doing some minor part of the job.

2   This rating indicates that this competency is desirable and useful for doing some minor part of the job but is not important to successfully meeting the major demands of the job.

3   This rating indicates that this competence is moderately important to successful job performance.

4   This rating indicates that this competence is very important to successful job performance.

   This rating indicates that this competence is critically important for successful job performance.

Template I.1 Senior Management/Executive Importance Ratings: Work Activities

Manage Strategic Planning

1 _____ Propose and/or review proposed strategies and objectives to be included in future business plans.

2 _____ Identify potential business opportunities and threats to current or future operations for incorporation in the overall strategy.

3 _____ Develop models to be used in market analysis and strategic planning.

4 _____ Analyze business conditions and competition regarding existing or planned company products, programs or planned operations.

5 _____ Assess and evaluate the adequacy of manpower resources, internal business controls, equipment, and facilities to meet present and future needs.

6 _____ Develop and maintain a network of external relationships in the business community and government to gain and share access to information about future changes impacting one's organization.

7 _____ Monitor financial and economic information regarding variables that affect business operations and investments.

8 _____ Examine reviews and predictions about companies, industries, the economy, and national trends for operational and strategic implications.

9 _____ Monitor the relevant literature in relevant fields to establish a base of information for strategic and operational purposes.

Manage Operations

10 _____ Set performance objectives for operating groups and monitor progress toward those objectives.

11 _____ Prepare or update reports on activities in specific areas of responsibility.

12 _____ Oversee operating procedures for individual units within the organization

13 _____ Monitor the design, installation, and evaluation of systems and procedures for quality control.

14 _____ Develop and implement methods and procedures for evaluating the performance of a department to identify when changes or improvements are needed.

15 _____ Analyze business operation or project requirements to determine individual roles and make work assignments.

(continues)

Template I.1 (Continued)

Plan, Organize, Schedule, Coordinate

16 _____ Review the status of work schedules, identifying factors requiring attention and needed adjustments in work activities.

17 _____ Adjust schedules to accommodate changes due to emergencies or other unanticipated events.

18 _____ Anticipate any possible short-term changes and identify adjustment necessary to address them.

19 _____ Coordinate project activities and set priorities to prevent duplication or schedule conflicts.

20 _____ Develop project action plans including costs, critical dates, and required activities for completion.

21 _____ Monitor and evaluate activity and progress on multiple projects to determine need for changing priorities and resource allocation.

Supervise Direct Reports

22 _____ Intervene to resolve disagreements, conflicts, and interpersonal difficulties among direct reports.

23 _____ Identify and address personal problems or deficiencies that affect job performance of direct reports.

24 _____ Establish and communicate performance goals and standards to direct reports to clarify job and organizational expectations and goals.

25 _____ Make recommendations for adjustments in compensation based on performance or change in job duties.

26 _____ Distribute work assignments to direct reports based on employee workload, skills, or organizational priorities.

27 _____ Compare subordinates' job performance against work standards and conduct regular performance reviews to provide feedback and develop future performance objectives.

Manage Public and Community Relations

28 _____ Represent the organization at public affairs, professional or industry conventions, and trade shows.

29 _____ Answer inquiries concerning available products, programs, or services.

30 _____ Organize public service functions of the organization, such as annual fund drives, community service activities, etc.

31 _____ Convey interests and concerns of community groups to the organization.

Template I.1 (Continued)

32 _____ Prepare and distribute fact sheets, news releases, photographs, or other information to media representatives or those interested in learning about the organization.

33 _____ Develop and promote goodwill through speeches, exhibits, films, tours, or discussion.

Consult Internally

34 _____ Give professional advice and specialized assistance on technical problems or in a specific area of business operations.

35 _____ When requested, provide expert counsel and guidance to colleagues in areas of expertise.

36 _____ Discuss a project with relevant others to define problem(s) and establish scope, design, and budget for the project.

Manage Regulatory Compliance

37 _____ Together with legal counsel, evaluate business activities and objectives in light of applicable laws or regulations.

38 _____ Draft statements to be signed by others that obligate or release the company from financial/ legal obligations.

39 _____ Monitor the work of independent auditors to verify results and conclusions.

40 _____ Oversee procedures to bring business operations into compliance with federal, state, and/or local laws.

41 _____ Monitor business operations to assess compliance with state and federal regulations or company policies.

42 _____ Provide liaison between legal counsel and the organization in investigations of alleged violations of local, state, or federal laws.

Manage Finances and Financial Systems

43 _____ Monitor expenditures to identify trends and evaluate variances from budget.

44 _____ Develop and justify a budget based on strategic and operating plans and forecasts of needs and costs.

45 _____ Conduct analyses and prepare estimates of project feasibility according to costs and benefits.

46 _____ Prepare and/or review contracts, purchase agreements, and other financial arrangements.

(continues)

Template I.1 (Continued)

47 _____ Develop and implement modifications in organizational procedures or work methods to correct or contain budget variances.

48 _____ Develop long-range budget projections and recommendations for financial management based on business plans and management directives.

Manage Information Systems

49 _____ Manage the identification of the type and the source of information and formats required for reports for comprehensive, accurate analysis and reporting of operations data.

49 _____ Identify weaknesses, problems, or irregularities in collection or analysis of data for various aspects of business operations.

50 _____ Review interpretation of data to identify patterns, trends, and irregularities in company operations.

51 _____ Oversee the development of data processing systems to support company, divisional, or department functions.

52 _____ Manage existing computer systems and programs for evidence of problems.

53 _____ Provide input concerning purchase of new computer equipment and/or software to improve data processing capabilities.

Manage Marketing

54 _____ Review analyses of customer requirements and market conditions to develop marketing strategies and plans.

55 _____ Supervise preparation of sales and marketing proposals.

56 _____ Oversee the design of advertising and promotional materials in accordance with marketing strategy and goals

57 _____ Review market penetration forecasts based on historical data, sales strategy, and competitor activity in each sales territory.

58 _____ Coordinate the development of programs to establish or increase branding, improve company or product image, product acceptance, etc.

59 _____ Oversee development of product marketing strategies including features to emphasize, benefits, price points, product mix, etc., based on market research and strategic goals.

60 _____ Review sales territories and market target areas to make any necessary adjustments.

Template I.1 (Continued)

61 _____ Apply sophisticated or technical procedures to analyze data and reach expert conclusions.

Manage Human Resources

62 _____ Oversee and participate as necessary and appropriate in employee orientation program.

63 _____ Develop personnel policies, procedures, rules and regulations and oversee their implementation.

64 _____ Oversee the conduct of exit interviews to determine causes for separation and ensure identification of trends that have policy or procedural implications.

65 _____ Supervise the operation of employee benefit systems, including coordination with external providers.

66 _____ Oversee the development of job classification and salary administration programs.

67 _____ Develop and manage implementation of systems for recruiting, hiring, performance appraisal, training, and other personnel activities.

68 _____ Manage employee counseling processes for job performance, career developmental opportunities, training needs, and individual development plans.

69 _____ Review and evaluate the effectiveness of training courses, seminars, and other employee developmental opportunities.

70 _____ Supervise planning for and presentation of training seminars, workshops, conferences, instructional materials, and other activities for employee training and development.

71 _____ Identify specific employee training needs required by introduction of new equipment or procedures, or resulting from reorganization of personnel.

72 _____ Oversee selection or development of training programs, including the content, media, and materials.

73 _____ Confer with representatives from external educational and training vendors regarding the development or purchase of programs to meet the needs of employees.

Manage Labor Relations

74 _____ Manage responses to employee grievances or labor relations issues.

(continues)

Template I.1 (Continued)

75 _____ Review personnel staffing policies and procedures to assess and evaluate compliance with federal, state, and local regulations.

76 _____ Oversee management representatives who meet to discuss and resolve employee issues, grievances, work assignments, working conditions, etc.

77 _____ Establish relationship with employee representatives (unions, professional associations, etc.).

78 _____ Monitor organizational grievance activity to assess actions and disposition of incidents and ensure compliance with organizational policies.

79 _____ Represent management in management/labor relations activities and/or negotiations.

Manage Facilities

80 _____ Monitor inspections of installations, buildings, equipment, or facilities to determine their operational status.

81 _____ Manage the maintenance, service, and repair of equipment and facilities.

82 _____ Recommend plant sites, scope, concept, and other characteristics of potential properties based on market analyses and business projections.

83 _____ Monitor the design of construction plans to ensure the feasibility and practicality of projects.

84 _____ Oversee the handling of requests for maintenance or repair services to determine type, nature, and priority of requests.

85 _____ Manage meetings with outside vendors, contractors, or consultants to discuss equipment needs, specifications, and capabilities.

Manage Materials

86 _____ Oversee the reviewing of inventory, accounting, and/or shipping reports or records for possible discrepancies.

87 _____ Monitor distribution system of supplies and equipment to determine whether materials are delivered when required.

88 _____ Monitor requisitions and inventory levels to evaluate purchasing and supply practices.

89 _____ Manage the inventory supplies/goods to determine operating costs and control stock shrinkage.

Template I.1 (Continued)

90 _____ Manage the placement of incoming supplies, equipment, and materials into prescribed storage areas.

91 _____ Review proposals from vendors on capital budget projects or major acquisitions of equipment, materials, or services and monitor the requisition process.

Manage Purchasing

92 _____ Supervise the solicitation of bids for acquiring major equipment, facilities, etc.

93 _____ Negotiate price, terms, and conditions of major contracts.

94 _____ Participate in contracting arrangement for major acquisitions.

Manage Safety and Security

95 _____ Oversee instruction of workers in safe working habits and on the hazards involved in equipment, materials, or processes.

96 _____ Manage inspections of buildings and equipment to evaluate maintenance needs, safety hazards, and legal compliance with federal, state, or local standards.

97 _____ Oversee development and implementation of safety/accident prevention programs for the work area.

98 _____ Investigate and document the events, pertinent conditions and actions taken with regard to accidents, thefts or other safety/security issues.

99 _____ Ensure development and installation of procedures for traffic control, building security, and protection of employees on company properties.

100 _____ Conduct or direct research to identify hazards and evaluate costs for various production activities.

Template I.2 Senior Management/Executive Importance Ratings: Competencies

Manage Strategic Planning

1 _____ Ability to lead a strategic planning effort to plan an organization's future courses of action.

2 _____ Knowledge of how to develop and implement a strategic plan.

3 _____ Ability to identify the important threats and opportunities confronting the organization.

4 _____ Ability to identify the key decision points and milestones in the implementation of the organization's strategic plan.

5 _____ Knowledge of the significant factors to be considered and how to weigh them when making strategic organizational decisions.

6 _____ Knowledge of pending or potential changes in external factors that may impact the fulfillment of the organization's mission.

7 _____ Knowledge of competitors' actions and plans that could impact the organization.

8 _____ Ability to identify the probable impact of current and pending federal, state, or local guidelines, regulations, and programs that may impact the organization's strategic plan.

Solve Problems

9 _____ Ability to recognize when and to specify what additional information is necessary to solve problems.

10 _____ Ability to evaluate data from multiple sources and integrate these data into recommendations.

11 _____ Ability to adapt data gathering approaches for solving different types of problems.

12 _____ Ability to recognize when significant new information questions an accepted solution to a problem so that additional analysis is required.

13 _____ Ability to determine the point at which a deviation from the expected is significant and indicates the existence of a problem.

14 _____ Ability to determine the required characteristics of an effective solution to a given problem.

15 _____ Ability to anticipate potential problems and act promptly to solve them early, before they become more serious.

16 _____ Ability to identify alternate solutions to scarcity in human or material resources that are necessary to sustain operations

Template I.2 (Continued)

17 _____ Ability to identify and prioritize requirements of operations to maintain management control and achieve the desired outcomes.

18 _____ Skill in identifying and/or modifying standard solutions to problems when unanticipated developments occur.

19 _____ Ability to identify obstacles to the flow of an activity and to identify and initiate alternative procedures to maintain continuity.

20 _____ Ability to react and provide action-oriented instructions and directions in emergency situations.

Plan, Organize, Schedule, and Coordinate

21 _____ Ability to schedule multiple activities or projects involving the availability of resources including materials, capital, and human resources.

22 _____ Ability to determine proper priorities and perspectives when managing multiple activities or projects.

23 _____ Ability to determine when, where, and how to establish and maintain management controls to monitor operations and projects.

24 _____ Ability to calculate human, material, and other resource requirements necessary to complete activities or projects.

25 _____ Ability to determine and implement the sequence of necessary steps in conducting a project or activity successfully.

26 _____ Ability to delegate assignments/responsibilities based on subordinate strengths, developmental needs, and workload.

27 _____ Ability to adjust one's pace of activity to keep up with rapidly occurring events or changing conditions and circumstances.

Supervise Direct Reports

28 _____ Ability to disregard one's personal feelings in the assignment of tasks or in the conduct of business activities.

29 _____ Ability to explain or illustrate work techniques to subordinates and provide them with performance feedback.

30 _____ Ability to conduct performance reviews of subordinates following and applying organizational requirements and standards.

31 _____ Ability to recognize situational constraints or conditions that affect choice of one's supervisory behavior or style.

(continues)

Template I.2 (Continued)

32 _____ Ability to persuade others to perform and complete activities not within own order of priorities.

33 _____ Ability to recognize situations or conditions subordinates would find rewarding.

Manage Public and Community Relations

34 _____ Ability to establish and maintain cordial relationships with media representatives.

35 _____ Skill in adapting presentations to audience requirements and the specific purposes of the presentation.

36 _____ Ability to identify and relate to key members of the community who represent or can influence different key stakeholders.

37 _____ Ability to develop and maintain sources of information in the community concerning the image of the organization.

38 _____ Skills in planning and conducting special events and employee activities.

39 _____ Skill in identifying topics, issues, or concerns with potential for conflict between the organization and various community or advocacy groups.

Manage Personal/Interpersonal Relations

40 _____ Ability to ignore personal likes and dislikes in dealing with others and focus on the desired outcome.

41 _____ Sensitivity to social and interpersonal cues in dealing with others and ability to utilize them to achieve organizational goals.

42 _____ Ability to build and maintain credibility in professional relations with customers, vendors, and others.

43 _____ Ability to absorb criticism and negative feedback while maintaining a balanced perspective on issues.

44 _____ Ability to explain policy and procedures to dissatisfied customers, employees, and other stakeholders without compromising organizational policy.

45 _____ Ability to provide feedback or objections to the views of others without personal accusations or acrimony.

46 _____ Ability to negotiate priorities and "make deals" with individuals in various parts of the organization in order to gain their cooperation and support for a project or activity.

Template I.2 (Continued)

Communicate Orally and in Writing

47 _____ Ability to prepare and deliver effective presentations.

48 _____ Ability to raise and sequence questions in order to obtain important information.

49 _____ Ability to summarize the comments, observations, activities, and opinions of others.

50 _____ Ability to develop a consensus after hearing disparate views.

51 _____ Ability to design a presentation that addresses the interests of the listeners and takes into account their level of understanding.

52 _____ Ability to identify the needs of various stakeholders for effective communication.

53 _____ Ability to select words that convey precisely one's purpose and to present ideas in an order that is clear to the listener.

54 _____ Ability to translate one's ideas into action-oriented memoranda.

55 _____ Ability to write high-quality reports that are logical, clear, and targeted to the audience.

56 _____ Ability to prepare technical reports for use by others who share one's technical background.

57 _____ Ability to communicate company policy or intent in contracts, letters, or other formal documents.

58 _____ Ability to translate or interpret technical information and prepare reports for use by others without a technical background.

59 _____ Ability to prepare clear instructions or directives in writing.

Adapt to Work and Organization Requirements

60 _____ Knowledge of organizational practices and norms regarding meetings, events, appointments, authority relationships, and organizational structure.

61 _____ Knowledge of the relationships, dependencies, and contingencies among organizational units, key management positions, and other positions and functions.

62 _____ Knowledge of the proprietary standards regarding discussion of company operations, plans, problems, and business and professional relations with other organizations.

(continues)

Template I.2   (Continued)

63 _____ Knowledge of the norms and practices regarding verbal expression and behavior in professional or social settings in which the individual is identified with the organization.

64 _____ Knowledge of the formal and informal standards regarding dress, language, personal hygiene, attendance, and expressed attitudes when identified with the organization.

65 _____ Ability to differentiate settings, conditions, or circumstances that determine when the individual is identified with the organization or is functioning as a private citizen.

Manage Finances and Financial Systems

66 _____ Ability to translate broad goals into required activities and identify cost estimates for labor, services, supplies, and equipment in order to develop a budget.

67 _____ Knowledge of interim reporting systems (e.g., monthly or year-to-date) to monitor compliance to budget.

68 _____ Knowledge of how accounting/financial information contributes to management understanding and decisions.

69 _____ Ability to analyze financial statements to locate the reasons for variances in specific operations.

70 _____ Knowledge of indicators used to assess the organization's operational effectiveness and financial condition.

71 _____ Ability to gather information obtained from economic indicators, trends, and business cycles and apply such information in forecasting.

Manage Information Systems

72 _____ Ability to identify the type and the source of information and formats required for reports.

73 _____ Ability to identify weaknesses, problems, or irregularities in collection or analysis of data for various business operations.

74 _____ Ability to review interpretation of data to identify patterns, trends, and irregularities in company operations.

75 _____ Knowledge to oversee the development of data processing systems to support company, divisional, or department functions.

76 _____ Ability to manage existing computer systems and programs for evidence of problems.

77 _____ Knowledge to provide input concerning purchase of new computer equipment and/or software to improve data processing capabilities.

Template I.2 (Continued)

Manage Marketing

78 _____ Ability to understand how the organization's products or services meet or fail to meet customer needs.

79 _____ Ability to analyze existing accounts or client relationships to determine the potential for further development.

80 _____ Ability to conceive and develop marketing campaigns to address potential market requirements.

81 _____ Ability to determine which features of a product should be stressed in marketing programs.

82 _____ Ability to determine desirable characteristics of possible markets to guide marketing efforts to prospect for and qualify customers.

83 _____ Ability to guide development of new or improved products or services based on emerging changes in customer needs or requirements.

Manage Human Resources

84 _____ Ability to generate relevant information in employment interviews for decision making.

85 _____ Knowledge of the relevant labor market and sources for recruiting potential employees for different jobs.

86 _____ Knowledge of federal, state, and local laws or guidelines about employee benefits packages.

87 _____ Ability to present and maintain the organization's positive image during the employment process.

88 _____ Ability to identify relevant applicant background and characteristics through reviews of resumes, application forms, etc.

89 _____ Ability to identify and address issues that have a significant impact on employee welfare and morale.

90 _____ Ability to counsel direct reports on their training and development needs in order to help them attain their career goals.

91 _____ Ability to identify a subordinate's strengths and weaknesses in order to develop a mentoring program.

92 _____ Knowledge of the availability, quality, and applicability of various internal and external training programs.

93 _____ Knowledge of training and development programs that will meet the requirements established in training needs analysis.

(continues)

Template I.2 (Continued)

94 _____ Ability to review and interpret evaluations of training and development effectiveness.

Manage Labor Relations

95 _____ Ability to identify issues that have a significant impact on existing or prospective employee contractual issues.

96 _____ Knowledge of procedures for handling and resolving grievances.

97 _____ Knowledge of federal, state, and local laws or regulations regarding employment practices and personnel actions.

98 _____ Knowledge of labor law and of pending legislation or litigation having implications for the organization.

99 _____ Ability to identify key issues for arbitration or contract negotiations.

100 _____ Ability to identify with management's point of view and to represent it in disagreements and in adversarial relationships.

Manage Facilities

101 _____ Ability to supervise the design of appropriate floor plans of physical plants for purposes of fire control, safety, and security.

102 _____ Knowledge of standard security and loss-prevention programs.

103 _____ Knowledge of the space and facilities requirements of different departments and operations.

104 _____ Knowledge of maintenance requirements of different types of physical facilities.

105 _____ Knowledge of routine and preventive maintenance required to maintain the operational status of operating equipment.

106 _____ Knowledge of standard safety and fire prevention programs.

Manage Materials

107 _____ Knowledge of how to review inventory, accounting, and/or shipping reports or records for possible discrepancies.

108 _____ Ability to monitor distribution system of supplies and equipment to determine whether materials are delivered when required.

109 _____ Skill in monitoring requisitions and inventory levels to evaluate purchasing and supply practices.

110 _____ Ability to manage the inventory supplies/goods to determine operating costs and control stock shrinkage.

111 _____ Ability to manage the placement of incoming supplies, equipment, and materials into prescribed storage areas.

Template I.2 (Continued)

112 _____ Ability to review proposals from vendors on capital budget projects or major acquisitions of equipment, materials, or services and monitor the requisition process.,

Manage Purchasing

113 _____ Knowledge of trends and pending changes in price or availability of commodities, supplies, equipment, or services required by the organization.

114 _____ Knowledge of standard procurement practices (e.g., bidding, contracting, purchase orders, etc.).

115 _____ Knowledge of the cost implications of problems with equipment or in operations.

116 _____ Knowledge of standard inventory control systems and monitoring procedures.

117 _____ Knowledge of required supplies and equipment for various types of manufacturing or business operations.

118 _____ Ability to negotiate prices, terms, and conditions with vendors favorable to company's position and interests.

Manage Safety and Security

119 _____ Knowledge of safe working habits and of the hazards involved in equipment, materials, or processes.

120 _____ Ability to manage inspections of buildings and equipment to evaluate maintenance needs, safety hazards, and legal compliance with federal, state, or local standards.

121 _____ Ability to oversee development and implementation of safety/accident prevention programs for the work area.

122 _____ Investigate and document the events, pertinent conditions, and actions taken with regard to accidents, thefts, or other safety/security issues.

123 _____ Ability to ensure development and installation of procedures for traffic control, building security, and protection of employees on company properties.

124 _____ Knowledge of how to conduct or direct research to identify hazards and evaluate costs for various production activities.

Appendix J

SUMMARY OF IMPORTANCE OF WORK ACTIVITIES AND COMPETENCIES

Target Job Title:_____

Location:_____ Date:_____

    This form provides a convenient way to summarize the ratings of the importance of the various work activities that have been identified by the selected raters as important on this particular job. In rating the importance of each work activity, the raters used the following rating scale:

Rating	Meaning of the Rating
0	This rating indicates that the work activity is never done and is not part of the job.
1	This rating indicates that the work activity has only minor importance relative to other activities performed by individuals in this job. Considering all activities, it would have the lowest priority or importance.
2	This rating indicates that the work activity has a relatively low level of importance compared to other job activities.
3	This rating indicates that the work activity is moderately important for fully effective job performance relative to other activities, and has about average priority among all activities performed.

4   This rating indicates that the work activity is very important to fully effective job performance. It has a higher degree of importance or priority than most other activities.

5   This rating indicates that the work activity is one of the few most essential activities performed. It is one of the most critical aspects of the job.

Ordinarily we are concerned only with importance ratings of "3" or higher. Any rating lower than "3" is unlikely to be an important descriptor of the job and can be safely ignored. Therefore we have provided summary forms for only the top three ratings—3, 4, and 5.

Each of the forms in this appendix contains a column for each item in the template, plus columns for recording each rater's assessment of that item. For example, using the summary form for Work Activities rated "5," the person completing the summary should simply go through the template completed by the first rater and place a check mark in the box for every item that received a "5" rating—one that indicated that this Work Activity was essential to performing this job. The summarizer should then do the same for those items rated "4" and then "3," using the appropriate summary form. The summary forms provided list the maximum number of items that can be rated in any of the standard templates. If any additional items have been added or more than eight raters are involved, additional copies of these forms can be duplicated.

After the Work Activities ratings are entered on the three summary forms, a similar process should be used to enter the competency ratings, using the provided summary forms. These ratings of both the work activities and job competencies can then be used in the writing of the job description.

Essential Work Activities Rated 5

Item	Rater 1	Rater 2	Rater 3	Rater 4	Rater 5	Rater 6	Rater 7	Rater 8
1								
2								
3								
4								
5								
6								
7								
8								
9								
10								
11								
12								
13								
14								
15								
16								
17								
18								
19								
20								
21								
22								
23								
24								
25								
26								
27								

(continues)

Essential Work Activities Rated 5 (Continued)

Item	Rater 1	Rater 2	Rater 3	Rater 4	Rater 5	Rater 6	Rater 7	Rater 8
28								
29								
30								
31								
32								
33								
34								
35								
36								
37								
38								
39								
40								
41								
42								
43								
44								
45								
46								
47								
48								
49								
50								
51								
52								
53								
54								
55								

Essential Work Activities Rated 5 (Continued)

Item	Rater 1	Rater 2	Rater 3	Rater 4	Rater 5	Rater 6	Rater 7	Rater 8
56								
57								
58								
59								
60								
61								
62								
63								
64								
65								
66								
67								
68								
69								
70								
71								
72								
73								
74								
75								
76								
77								
78								
79								
80								
81								

(continues)

Essential Work Activities Rated 5 (Continued)

Item	Rater 1	Rater 2	Rater 3	Rater 4	Rater 5	Rater 6	Rater 7	Rater 8
82								
83								
84								
85								
86								
87								
88								
89								
90								
01								
92								
93								
94								
95								
96								
97								
98								
99								
100								
101								
102								
103								
104								
105								
106								
107								
108								

Essential Work Activities Rated 5 (Continued)

Item	Rater 1	Rater 2	Rater 3	Rater 4	Rater 5	Rater 6	Rater 7	Rater 8
109								
110								
111								
112								
113								
114								
115								
116								
117								
118								
119								
120								
121								
122								
123								
124								
125								

Very Important Work Activities Rated 4

Item	Rater 1	Rater 2	Rater 3	Rater 4	Rater 5	Rater 6	Rater 7	Rater 8
1								
2								
3								
4								
5								
6								
7								
8								
9								
10								
11								
12								
13								
14								
15								
16								
17								
18								
19								
20								
21								
22								
23								
24								
25								
26								
27								
28								

Very Important Work Activities Rated 4 (Continued)

Item	Rater 1	Rater 2	Rater 3	Rater 4	Rater 5	Rater 6	Rater 7	Rater 8
29								
30								
31								
32								
33								
34								
35								
36								
37								
38								
39								
40								
41								
42								
43								
44								
45								
46								
47								
48								
49								
50								
51								
52								
53								
54								

(continues)

Very Important Work Activities Rated 4 (Continued)

Item	Rater 1	Rater 2	Rater 3	Rater 4	Rater 5	Rater 6	Rater 7	Rater 8
55								
56								
57								
58								
59								
60								
61								
62								
63								
64								
65								
66								
67								
68								
69								
70								
71								
72								
73								
74								
75								
76								
77								
78								
79								
80								
81								
82								

Very Important Work Activities Rated 4 (Continued)

Item	Rater 1	Rater 2	Rater 3	Rater 4	Rater 5	Rater 6	Rater 7	Rater 8
83								
84								
85								
86								
87								
88								
89								
90								
01								
92								
93								
94								
95								
96								
97								
98								
99								
100								
101								
102								
103								
104								
105								
106								
107								
108								

(continues)

Very Important Work Activities Rated 4 (Continued)

Item	Rater 1	Rater 2	Rater 3	Rater 4	Rater 5	Rater 6	Rater 7	Rater 8
109								
110								
111								
112								
113								
114								
115								
116								
117								
118								
119								
120								
121								
122								
123								
124								
125								

Moderately Important Work Activities Rated 3

Item	Rater 1	Rater 2	Rater 3	Rater 4	Rater 5	Rater 6	Rater 7	Rater 8
1								
2								
3								
4								
5								
6								
7								
8								
9								
10								
11								
12								
13								
14								
15								
16								
17								
18								
19								
20								
21								
22								
23								
24								
25								
26								
27								

(continues)

Moderately Important Work Activities Rated 3 (Continued)

Item	Rater 1	Rater 2	Rater 3	Rater 4	Rater 5	Rater 6	Rater 7	Rater 8
28								
29								
30								
31								
32								
33								
34								
35								
36								
37								
38								
39								
40								
41								
42								
43								
44								
45								
46								
47								
48								
49								
50								
51								
52								
53								
54								
55								

Moderately Important Work Activities Rated 3 (Continued)

Item	Rater 1	Rater 2	Rater 3	Rater 4	Rater 5	Rater 6	Rater 7	Rater 8
56								
57								
58								
59								
60								
61								
62								
63								
64								
65								
66								
67								
68								
69								
70								
71								
72								
73								
74								
75								
76								
77								
78								
79								
80								
81								

(continues)

Moderately Important Work Activities Rated 3 (Continued)

Item	Rater 1	Rater 2	Rater 3	Rater 4	Rater 5	Rater 6	Rater 7	Rater 8
82								
83								
84								
85								
86								
87								
88								
89								
90								
01								
92								
93								
94								
95								
96								
97								
98								
99								
100								
101								
102								
103								
104								
105								
106								
107								
108								

Moderately Important Work Activities Rated 3 (Continued)

Item	Rater 1	Rater 2	Rater 3	Rater 4	Rater 5	Rater 6	Rater 7	Rater 8
109								
110								
111								
112								
113								
114								
115								
116								
117								
118								
119								
120								
121								
122								
123								
124								
125								

Summary of Competencies Importance Ratings

Target Job Title:_____

Location:_____ Date:_____

This form provides a convenient way to summarize the ratings of the importance of the various competencies that have been identified by the selected raters as important on this particular job. In rating the importance of each work activity, the raters used the following rating scale:

Rating	Meaning of the Rating
0	This rating indicates that this competency is not necessary for job performance.
1	This rating indicates that this competency has only minor or incidental importance for effective job performance. It is not essential to doing the job, but may occasionally be useful for doing some minor part of the job.
2	This rating indicates that this competency is desirable and useful for doing some minor part of the job but is not important to successfully meeting the major demands of the job.
3	This rating indicates that this competence is moderately important to successful job performance.
4	This rating indicates that this competence is very important to successful job performance.
	This rating indicates that this competence is critically important for successful job performance.

Ordinarily we are concerned only with importance ratings of "3" or higher. Any rating lower than 3 is unlikely to be an important competence for success on this job and can be safely ignored. Therefore we have provided summary forms for only the top three ratings—3, 4, and 5.

Each of these forms contains a column for each item in the template plus columns for recording each rater's assessment of that item. For example, using the summary form for competencies rated 5, the person completing the summary should simply go through the template completed by the first rater, and place a check mark in the box for every item that received a 5 rating—one that indicated that this competence was essential to performing this job. The summarizer should then do the same for those items rated 4 and then 3, using the appropriate summary form. The summary forms provided list the maximum number of items that can be rated in any of the standard templates. If any additional items have been added or more than eight raters are involved, additional copies of these forms can be duplicated.

Essential Competencies Rated 5

Item	Rater 1	Rater 2	Rater 3	Rater 4	Rater 5	Rater 6	Rater 7	Rater 8
1								
2								
3								
4								
5								
6								
7								
8								
9								
10								
11								
12								
13								
14								
15								
16								
17								
18								
19								
20								
21								
22								
23								
24								
25								
26								
27								
28								

Essential Competencies Rated 5 (Continued)

Item	Rater 1	Rater 2	Rater 3	Rater 4	Rater 5	Rater 6	Rater 7	Rater 8
29								
30								
31								
32								
33								
34								
35								
36								
37								
38								
39								
40								
41								
42								
43								
44								
45								
46								
47								
48								
49								
50								
51								
52								
53								
54								

(continues)

Essential Competencies Rated 5 (Continued)

Item	Rater 1	Rater 2	Rater 3	Rater 4	Rater 5	Rater 6	Rater 7	Rater 8
55								
56								
57								
58								
59								
60								
61								
62								
63								
64								
65								
66								
67								
68								
69								
70								
71								
72								
73								
74								
75								
76								
77								
78								
79								
80								
81								
82								

Essential Competencies Rated 5 (Continued)

Item	Rater 1	Rater 2	Rater 3	Rater 4	Rater 5	Rater 6	Rater 7	Rater 8
83								
84								
85								
86								
87								
88								
89								
90								
01								
92								
93								
94								
95								
96								
97								
98								
99								
100								
101								
102								
103								
104								
105								
106								
107								
108								

(continues)

Essential Competencies Rated 5 (Continued)

Item	Rater 1	Rater 2	Rater 3	Rater 4	Rater 5	Rater 6	Rater 7	Rater 8
109								
110								
111								
112								
113								
114								
115								
116								
117								
118								
119								
120								
121								
122								
123								
124								
125								

Very Important Competencies Rated 4

Item	Rater 1	Rater 2	Rater 3	Rater 4	Rater 5	Rater 6	Rater 7	Rater 8
1								
2								
3								
4								
5								
6								
7								
8								
9								
10								
11								
12								
13								
14								
15								
16								
17								
18								
19								
20								
21								
22								
23								
24								
25								
26								
27								

(continues)

Very Important Competencies Rated 4 (Continued)

Item	Rater 1	Rater 2	Rater 3	Rater 4	Rater 5	Rater 6	Rater 7	Rater 8
28								
29								
30								
31								
32								
33								
34								
35								
36								
37								
38								
39								
40								
41								
42								
43								
44								
45								
46								
47								
48								
49								
50								
51								
52								
53								
54								
55								

Very Important Competencies Rated 4 (Continued)

Item	Rater 1	Rater 2	Rater 3	Rater 4	Rater 5	Rater 6	Rater 7	Rater 8
56								
57								
58								
59								
60								
61								
62								
63								
64								
65								
66								
67								
68								
69								
70								
71								
72								
73								
74								
75								
76								
77								
78								
79								
80								
81								

(continues)

Very Important Competencies Rated 4 (Continued)

Item	Rater 1	Rater 2	Rater 3	Rater 4	Rater 5	Rater 6	Rater 7	Rater 8
82								
83								
84								
85								
86								
87								
88								
89								
90								
01								
92								
93								
94								
95								
96								
97								
98								
99								
100								
101								
102								
103								
104								
105								
106								
107								
108								

Very Important Competencies Rated 4 (Continued)

Item	Rater 1	Rater 2	Rater 3	Rater 4	Rater 5	Rater 6	Rater 7	Rater 8
109								
110								
111								
112								
113								
114								
115								
116								
117								
118								
119								
120								
121								
122								
123								
124								
125								

Moderately Important Competencies Rated 3

Item	Rater 1	Rater 2	Rater 3	Rater 4	Rater 5	Rater 6	Rater 7	Rater 8
1								
2								
3								
4								
5								
6								
7								
8								
9								
10								
11								
12								
13								
14								
15								
16								
17								
18								
19								
20								
21								
22								
23								
24								
25								
26								
27								
28								

Moderately Important Competencies Rated 3 (Continued)

Item	Rater 1	Rater 2	Rater 3	Rater 4	Rater 5	Rater 6	Rater 7	Rater 8
29								
30								
31								
32								
33								
34								
35								
36								
37								
38								
39								
40								
41								
42								
43								
44								
45								
46								
47								
48								
49								
50								
51								
52								
53								
54								

(continues)

Moderately Important Competencies Rated 3 (Continued)

Item	Rater 1	Rater 2	Rater 3	Rater 4	Rater 5	Rater 6	Rater 7	Rater 8
55								
56								
57								
58								
59								
60								
61								
62								
63								
64								
65								
66								
67								
68								
69								
70								
71								
72								
73								
74								
75								
76								
77								
78								
79								
80								
81								
82								

Moderately Important Competencies Rated 3 (Continued)

Item	Rater 1	Rater 2	Rater 3	Rater 4	Rater 5	Rater 6	Rater 7	Rater 8
83								
84								
85								
86								
87								
88								
89								
90								
01								
92								
93								
94								
95								
96								
97								
98								
99								
100								
101								
102								
103								
104								
105								
106								
107								
108								

(*continues*)

Moderately Important Competencies Rated 3 (Continued)

Item	Rater 1	Rater 2	Rater 3	Rater 4	Rater 5	Rater 6	Rater 7	Rater 8
109								
110								
111								
112								
113								
114								
115								
116								
117								
118								
119								
120								
121								
122								
123								
124								
125								

Appendix K

WORKPLACE CHARACTERISTICS PROFILE

This profile has been designed to identify the priorities and the emphases that management places on doing work in this organization. The Workplace Characteristics Profile is intended for employees at all levels in the organization as a means for describing their views on how work is expected to be performed. As such, there are no right or wrong answers. Please follow the instructions for responding and be sure not to skip any of the questions.

In this questionnaire you are asked to consider the following statements that may describe the conditions or characteristics of the setting in which you work. You may know or learn these things in various ways, such as through direct communication, experience on the job, observation, or even lack of response to something you do on the job.

Use the following code to indicate the emphasis or priority of each statement or the extent to which the condition exists or describes the work setting. Please indicate your response to each statement and record your answers in the space provided.

0   Never emphasized or is not a priority in this work setting.

1   Occasionally emphasized or is a priority in this work setting.

2   Sometimes emphasized or is a priority in this work setting.

3   Quite often emphasized or is a priority in this work setting.

4   Frequently emphasized or is a priority in this work setting.

5   Always emphasized or is a priority in this work setting

_____   1. This job requires giving attention to many different problems or tasks each day.

_____   2. Work assignments on this job are made on the basis of a person's skills and abilities

_____   3. It doesn't take long before I find out how well or poorly I've done something on my job.

_____   4. In this job persons from different backgrounds can readily fit in.

_____   5. Written statements of procedures and policies are readily available to me in my job.

_____   6. In this job the gender of workers makes little or no difference.

_____   7. In this job I am expected to perform the same tasks in the same way.

_____   8. It is difficult for me and others to keep up with the changes in this job.

_____   9. I am expected to maintain efficiency of operations while accommodating changing conditions.

_____   10. It's inappropriate to make jokes at others' expense.

_____   11. I am expected to send proposed actions and recommend decisions to management for approval.

_____ 12. My performance is evaluated in terms of available, objective work standards.

_____ 13. I am expected to modify methods or change what I am doing to meet different conditions.

_____ 14. On this job no one pays much attention to any physical or mental limitations that a person may have.

_____ 15. I have little difficulty obtaining the information I need to do my job.

_____ 16. People from different backgrounds are expected to perform at the same level as others.

_____ 17. I accommodate and apply organizational rules and procedures in performing my job.

_____ 18. There is no "glass ceiling" for women on this job.

_____ 19. In this job I know what to do by looking at the available relevant information.

_____ 20. My job has changed and it is clear that these changes will benefit me.

_____ 21. I am expected to manage for current effectiveness mainly on conditions outside the organization, such as the market or competition.

_____ 22. In this job there's a good bit of emphasis on being "politically correct."

_____ 23. Professional and technical guidelines and standards limit my discretion in the way my work is accomplished.

_____ 24. I initiate work and follow through from beginning to end.

_____ 25. Most facets of the work in my area are measured and the results are available as trends or periodic summaries.

_____ 26. On this job there is a real attempt to accommodate persons who have physical or mental limitations.

_____ 27. I am expected to obtain information from others to help solve problems I encounter in my work.

_____ 28. Persons from different backgrounds quickly fit in with the others on this job.

_____ 29. In this job I have procedures to follow that are specified for each situation.

_____ 30. It is possible for both men and women to successfully perform this job.

_____ 31. I am faced with problems that demand so much time and attention that performance of my other duties must be delayed.

_____ 32. Even though I work hard to keep up with the changing demands of this job, I feel that I am falling behind and am at risk of losing my job.

_____ 33. In this position I must ask others or decide for myself how a task or situation should be handled and rely only rarely on written sets of instructions.

_____ 34. There's nothing wrong with telling an off-color joke now and then.

_____ 35. I am not likely to be promoted outside my area of specialization.

_____ 36. I receive support from my superiors whenever I need to try out new ideas to solve problems.

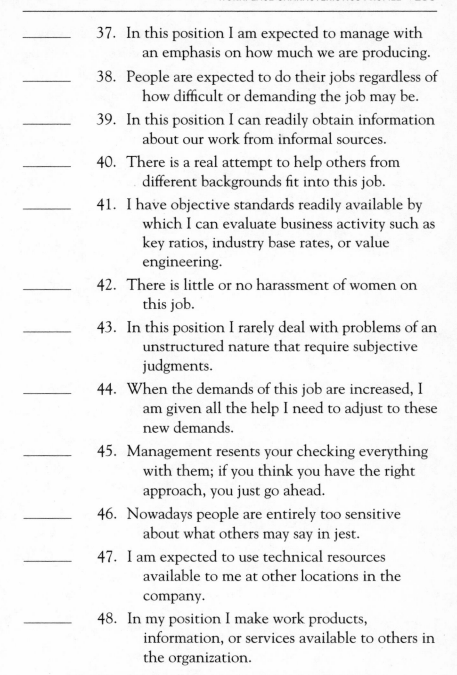

_____ 37. In this position I am expected to manage with an emphasis on how much we are producing.

_____ 38. People are expected to do their jobs regardless of how difficult or demanding the job may be.

_____ 39. In this position I can readily obtain information about our work from informal sources.

_____ 40. There is a real attempt to help others from different backgrounds fit into this job.

_____ 41. I have objective standards readily available by which I can evaluate business activity such as key ratios, industry base rates, or value engineering.

_____ 42. There is little or no harassment of women on this job.

_____ 43. In this position I rarely deal with problems of an unstructured nature that require subjective judgments.

_____ 44. When the demands of this job are increased, I am given all the help I need to adjust to these new demands.

_____ 45. Management resents your checking everything with them; if you think you have the right approach, you just go ahead.

_____ 46. Nowadays people are entirely too sensitive about what others may say in jest.

_____ 47. I am expected to use technical resources available to me at other locations in the company.

_____ 48. In my position I make work products, information, or services available to others in the organization.

_____ 49. I must take into account variances in delivery schedules of products or services from outside vendors in the day-to-day conduct of the job.

_____ 50. By and large, people here understand the limitations that others may have.

_____ 51. I know where to go for information that I need to perform my job.

_____ 52. It bothers me how others on this job think and talk.

_____ 53. The emphasis in this job is on managing current business operations to maintain continuous functioning.

_____ 54. Both men and women can readily perform this job.

_____ 55. The activities of my job are different on a day-to-day, week-to-week, or month-to-month basis.

_____ 56. This organization has really changed and I no longer feel I am an essential part of the organization

_____ 57. The emphasis in this job is on managing future changes in terms of bringing in new products, changing technology, or changing business strategy.

_____ 58. Teasing others on the job is inappropriate, even if it's to help make the time pass.

_____ 59. I am expected to be responsible for the achievement of goals that are part of my job.

_____ 60. The work performed on this job is directly related to the accomplishment of organization goals.

Scoring for the Workplace Characteristics Profile

To score the WCP, transfer the ratings to the table below and compute a total score for each scale.

Totals

1. _____	13. _____	25. _____	37. _____	49. _____	_____
2. _____	14. _____	26. _____	38. _____	50. _____	_____
3. _____	15. _____	27. _____	39. _____	51. _____	_____
4. _____	16. _____	28. _____	40. _____	52. _____	_____
5. _____	17. _____	29. _____	41. _____	53. _____	_____
6. _____	18. _____	30. _____	42. _____	54. _____	_____
7. _____	19. _____	31. _____	43. _____	55. _____	_____
8. _____	20. _____	32. _____	44. _____	56. _____	_____
9. _____	21. _____	33. _____	45. _____	57. _____	_____
10. _____	22. _____	34. _____	46. _____	58. _____	_____
11. _____	23. _____	35. _____	47. _____	59. _____	_____
12. _____	24. _____	36. _____	48. _____	60. _____	_____

Each of the Totals should then be entered in the graph below to provide a pictorial representation of the data.

Interpreting the Workplace Characteristics Profile

Managing Work Efficiently

Emphasis is on the efficient management of work in an increasingly dynamic and complex environment. Effectiveness of work performed is evidenced by the quality and quantity of output, and individuals are expected to adapt and orchestrate their activities on a relatively continuous basis in order to maintain efficiency. High scores on this factor indicate a strong focus on efficiency throughout the workplace.

Accommodating to Persons with Disabilities

Emphasis is on accommodating persons with disabilities. There is a focus on assisting individuals to overcome limitations and on facilitating individuals' efforts to overcome workplace obstacles. High scores indicate a focus on what individuals can do, how they can do it, and the adaptations and accommodations required by others for effective workplace functioning.

Communicating with Others

Emphasis is on communicating with others and seeking job-related information to increase both efficiency and effectiveness. Such information may come from a variety of sources—the work or work products, formal or informal contact—and is generally easily accessible. High scores indicate that individuals are expected to coordinate and communicate with others in order to obtain information for improving the quality and quantity of output.

Accommodating to Persons from Different Backgrounds

The emphasis is on adapting to people who do not come from the mainstream, but rather from the evolving heterogeneity of the workplace. Such persons come from different cultures and are different in their appearance, dress, attitudes, speech, and so on, and they often need acceptance and support to be successful in the workplace. High scores on this factor indicate a commitment to providing such acceptance and support.

Standardization of Work Roles and Procedures

Emphasis is on standardization of work roles and procedures. It exemplifies the classical bureaucratic characteristic of role standardization in which individuals know what they should do and know what is expected of them, and thus produce a continuity of activities. Individuals can predict accurately what is going to happen and how they are expected to react. High scores on this factor suggest a commitment to a bureaucratic approach to management.

Promoting Gender Equality

Emphasis is on providing equal treatment of men and women in the workplace—in job assignments, promotional opportunities, access to training, equality in pay and benefits, and all other important aspects of work. High scores on this factor indicate that there is clear support by management for a zero-tolerance policy of discrimination on the basis of gender.

Standardizing Tasks and Performance

Emphasis is on standardizing tasks and standardized performance of these job tasks. High scores on this factor indicate that tasks must be performed in a specified manner and that standardized approaches are required. High scores indicate that these are significant characteristics of the workplace and the individual has little discretion about managing his or her performance.

Managing Change

Emphasis is on providing support for employees in understanding the need for change, in coping with change, and in embarking on the many transitions required by changing conditions in the workplace. High scores indicate a generalized understanding that the environment is in a state of constant flux and that everyone needs to be prepared to adapt to these changes.

Managing Work for Effectiveness

Emphasis is on responding effectively to external forces. This approach is characterized by a focus on responding promptly to market changes, including customer wants and needs, other market shifts, competition, changing technology, laws and regulations. High scores on this scale suggest that persons are empowered to act without precedent and without guidance from others.

Controlling Harassment

Emphasis is on active discouragement of workplace harassment, intentional or unintentional, harassment based on race, age, gender, sexual orientation, physical limitation, or religion. There is clear support by management of a zero-tolerance policy against any form of workplace harassment.

Promoting Specialization

Emphasis is on developing and using a specialized skill that is regularly used on the job. This promotion of specialization precludes members of a work group from being cross-trained or alternating task assignments. High scores indicate that this bureaucratic approach prevents taking independent action to solve problems.

Promoting Independence of Action

Emphasis is on exercising independence of action. Individuals are expected to perform relatively independently and are held accountable through meeting output expectations and maintaining a high level of expertise. High scores indicate that individuals are encouraged to exercise initiative and take risks.

Index

Page references followed by *fig* indicate an illustrated figure; followed by *t* indicate a table.

About the Authors

Erich P. Prien, Ph.D., is an industrial and organizational psychologist specializing in the development, standardization, and application of psychological tests, especially in the workplace. He is the founder and president of Performance Management Press and the co-author of *Individual Assessment* (Pfeiffer, 2006).

Leonard D. Goodstein, Ph.D., is a consulting psychologist specializing in personality assessment, especially in the workplace— as well as executive development and coaching. He is a principal with Psichometrics International, LLC, and the co-author of *Individual Assessment* and *Applied Strategic Planning: The Consultant's Tool Kit* (Pfeiffer, 2008).

Jeanette Goodstein, Ph.D., is an organizational consultant and writer specializing in working with governmental and non-profit organizations. She is the co-author of the award-winning *Who's Driving Your Bus* and *Applied Strategic Planning: The Consultant's Tool Kit.*

Louis G. Gamble, Jr., Ed. D., is a consultant and entrepreneur specializing in the application of information technology to organizational change. He is a principal with Inclusive Marketing Consultants, LLC, and a frequent contributor to the professional literature.

Pfeiffer Publications Guide

This guide is designed to familiarize you with the various types of Pfeiffer publications. The formats section describes the various types of products that we publish; the methodologies section describes the many different ways that content might be provided within a product. We also provide a list of the topic areas in which we publish.

FORMATS

In addition to its extensive book-publishing program, Pfeiffer offers content in an array of formats, from fieldbooks for the practitioner to complete, ready-to-use training packages that support group learning.

FIELDBOOK Designed to provide information and guidance to practitioners in the midst of action. Most fieldbooks are companions to another, sometimes earlier, work, from which its ideas are derived; the fieldbook makes practical what was theoretical in the original text. Fieldbooks can certainly be read from cover to cover. More likely, though, you'll find yourself bouncing around following a particular theme, or dipping in as the mood, and the situation, dictate.

HANDBOOK A contributed volume of work on a single topic, comprising an eclectic mix of ideas, case studies, and best practices sourced by practitioners and experts in the field.

An editor or team of editors usually is appointed to seek out contributors and to evaluate content for relevance to the topic. Think of a handbook not as a ready-to-eat meal, but as a cookbook of ingredients that enables you to create the most fitting experience for the occasion.

RESOURCE Materials designed to support group learning. They come in many forms: a complete, ready-to-use exercise (such as a game); a comprehensive resource on one topic (such as conflict management) containing a variety of methods and approaches; or a collection of like-minded activities (such as icebreakers) on multiple subjects and situations.

TRAINING PACKAGE An entire, ready-to-use learning program that focuses on a particular topic or skill. All packages comprise a guide for the facilitator/trainer and a workbook for the participants. Some packages are supported with additional media—such as video—or learning aids, instruments, or other devices to help participants understand concepts or practice and develop skills.

- *Facilitator/trainer's guide* Contains an introduction to the program, advice on how to organize and facilitate the learning event, and step-by-step instructor notes. The guide also contains copies of presentation materials—handouts, presentations, and overhead designs, for example—used in the program.

- *Participant's workbook* Contains exercises and reading materials that support the learning goal and serves as a valuable reference and support guide for participants in the weeks and months that follow the learning event. Typically, each participant will require his or her own workbook.

ELECTRONIC CD-ROMs and web-based products transform static Pfeiffer content into dynamic, interactive experiences. Designed to take advantage of the searchability, automation, and ease-of-use that technology provides, our e-products bring convenience and immediate accessibility to your workspace.

METHODOLOGIES

CASE STUDY A presentation, in narrative form, of an actual event that has occurred inside an organization. Case studies are not prescriptive, nor are they used to prove a point; they are designed to develop critical analysis and decision-making skills. A case study has a specific time frame, specifies a sequence of events, is narrative in structure, and contains a plot structure—an issue (what should be/have been done?). Use case studies when the goal is to enable participants to apply previously learned theories to the circumstances in the case, decide what is pertinent, identify the real issues, decide what should have been done, and develop a plan of action.

ENERGIZER A short activity that develops readiness for the next session or learning event. Energizers are most commonly used after a break or lunch to stimulate or refocus the group. Many involve some form of physical activity, so they are a useful way to counter post-lunch lethargy. Other uses include transitioning from one topic to another, where "mental" distancing is important.

EXPERIENTIAL LEARNING ACTIVITY (ELA) A facilitator-led intervention that moves participants through the learning cycle from experience to application (also known as a Structured Experience). ELAs are carefully thought-out designs in which there is a definite learning purpose and intended outcome. Each step—everything that participants do during the activity—facilitates the accomplishment of the stated goal. Each ELA includes complete instructions for facilitating the intervention and a clear statement of goals, suggested group size and timing, materials required, an explanation of the process, and, where appropriate, possible variations to the activity. (For more detail on Experiential Learning Activities, see the Introduction to the *Reference Guide to Handbooks and Annuals*, 1999 edition, Pfeiffer, San Francisco.)

GAME A group activity that has the purpose of fostering team spirit and togetherness in addition to the achievement of a pre-stated goal. Usually contrived—undertaking a desert expedition, for example—this type of learning method offers an engaging means for participants to demonstrate and practice business and interpersonal skills. Games are effective for team building and personal development mainly because the goal is subordinate to the process—the means through which participants reach decisions, collaborate, communicate, and generate trust and understanding. Games often engage teams in "friendly" competition.

ICEBREAKER A (usually) short activity designed to help participants overcome initial anxiety in a training session and/or to acquaint the participants with one another. An icebreaker can be a fun activity or can be tied to specific topics or training goals. While a useful tool in itself, the icebreaker comes into its own in situations where tension or resistance exists within a group.

INSTRUMENT A device used to assess, appraise, evaluate, describe, classify, and summarize various aspects of human behavior. The term used to describe an instrument depends primarily on its format and purpose. These terms include survey, questionnaire, inventory, diagnostic, survey, and poll. Some uses of instruments include providing instrumental feedback to group members, studying here-and-now processes or functioning within a group, manipulating group composition, and evaluating outcomes of training and other interventions.

Instruments are popular in the training and HR field because, in general, more growth can occur if an individual is provided with a method for focusing specifically on his or her own behavior. Instruments also are used to obtain information that will serve as a basis for change and to assist in workforce planning efforts.

Paper-and-pencil tests still dominate the instrument landscape with a typical package comprising a facilitator's guide, which offers advice on administering the instrument and interpreting the collected data, and an initial set of instruments. Additional instruments are available separately. Pfeiffer, though, is investing heavily in e-instruments. Electronic instrumentation provides effortless distribution and, for larger groups particularly, offers advantages over paper-and-pencil tests in the time it takes to analyze data and provide feedback.

LECTURETTE A short talk that provides an explanation of a principle, model, or process that is pertinent to the participants' current learning needs. A lecturette is intended to establish a common language bond between the trainer and the participants by providing a mutual frame of reference. Use a lecturette as an introduction to a group activity or event, as an interjection during an event, or as a handout.

MODEL A graphic depiction of a system or process and the relationship among its elements. Models provide a frame of reference and something more tangible, and more easily remembered, than a verbal explanation. They also give participants something to "go on," enabling them to track their own progress as they experience the dynamics, processes, and relationships being depicted in the model.

ROLE PLAY A technique in which people assume a role in a situation/scenario: a customer service rep in an angry-customer exchange, for example. The way in which the role is approached is then discussed and feedback is offered. The role play is often repeated using a different approach and/or incorporating changes made based on feedback received. In other words, role playing is a spontaneous interaction involving realistic behavior under artificial (and safe) conditions.

SIMULATION A methodology for understanding the interrelationships among components of a system or process. Simulations differ from games in that they test or use a model that depicts or mirrors some aspect of reality in form, if not necessarily in content. Learning occurs by studying the effects of change on one or more factors of the model. Simulations are commonly used to test hypotheses about what happens in a system—often referred to as "what if?" analysis—or to examine best-case/worst-case scenarios.

THEORY A presentation of an idea from a conjectural perspective. Theories are useful because they encourage us to examine behavior and phenomena through a different lens.

TOPICS

The twin goals of providing effective and practical solutions for workforce training and organization development and meeting the educational needs of training and human resource professionals shape Pfeiffer's publishing program. Core topics include the following:

    Leadership & Management

    Communication & Presentation

    Coaching & Mentoring

    Training & Development

    E-Learning

    Teams & Collaboration

    OD & Strategic Planning

    Human Resources

    Consulting

What will you find on pfeiffer.com?

- The best in workplace performance solutions for training and HR professionals

- Downloadable training tools, exercises, and content

- Web-exclusive offers

- Training tips, articles, and news

- Seamless on-line ordering

- Author guidelines, information on becoming a Pfeiffer Affiliate, and much more

Discover more at www.pfeiffer.com